Am I My Brother's Keeper?

And Other Sermons that Matter

Scott D. Nowack

Parson's Porch Books
www.parsonsporchbooks.com

Am I My Brother's Keeper?

ISBN: Softcover 978-1-951472-09-2

Copyright © 2019 by Scott D. Nowack

Am I My Brother's Keeper?

Contents

Sermons Matter

Parson's Porch Books is delighted to present to you this series called Sermons Matter.

We believe that many of the best writers are pastors who take the role of preacher seriously. Week in, and week out, they exegete scripture, research material, write and deliver sermons in the context of the life of their particular congregation in their given community.

We further believe that sermons are extensions of Holy Scripture which need to be published beyond the manuscripts which are written for delivery each Sunday. Books serve as a vehicle for the sermon to continue to proclaim the Good News of the Morning to a broader audience.

Scott D. Nowack exemplifies the pastor who takes his sermons seriously week in and week out. His skills, both in crafting and writing, as a preacher are obvious.

We celebrate the wonderful occasion of the preaching event in Christian worship when the Pastor speaks, the People listen and the Work of the Church proceeds.

Take, Read, and Heed.

David Russell Tullock, M.Div., D.Min.
Publisher
Parson's Porch Books

Am I My Brother's Keeper?
Genesis 4:6-9 and Romans 2:1-11

Will you pray with me?

Loving and gracious God,

We have come from far and wide to this special place to hear your Word for us. Grant us the ears to hear, the minds to know, and the hearts to understand your message for us. Speak the truth and challenge our assumptions. Meet us at our point of need as we discern and understand our call to love and serve you and our neighbors with care, love and grace. Amen.

The question I wish to put before us tonight is: Am I my brother's keeper? This is not a Presbyterian question or a Lutheran question or even an Episcopalian question. This question has been discussed and written about for generations in both Jewish and Christian religious circles. It is biblical question pertinent to each of our lives as members of the human race. What does it mean to be my brother's keeper?

It is clear to me that Cain believe he was "the keeper of himself" and not "a keeper of his brother" or "his brother's keeper". We as a nation have been more concerned about meeting our own needs at the expense of the needs of others. Since 1980, our nation overall enjoyed the greatest period of economic expansion in our history. We were riding high on unprecedented economic growth. The stock market expanded and grew to unprecedented new highs. Aside from some minor slowdowns, it was an amazing time, as far as our material prosperity was concerned. But I believe it was also a time of great emptiness, scandal, pettiness, and greed. Our society strived for things that can only fill us for a moment. When the moment passed, we got bored with it and would buy something else or try to be someone else. We thought we had it all, that the good times would never end. We became complacent, self-assured, arrogant, and conceited in our prosperity.

This prosperity blinded our hearts. We were pre-occupied with me, myself and I. It was about how much I had, how much equity can I get out of my home, and soon greed and selfishness took hold of us. In the midst of this prosperity, "Am I my brother's keeper?" was not a popular question or idea to consider.

There was a brief time when we noticed the needs of others. The catastrophic events of September 11, 2001 touched all of us and profoundly changed our nation's psyche. I remember in the days following 9-11 the response to help was incredible! Not only from churches and synagogues, but from corporations and businesses of all sizes; help not only came from the New York and D.C. areas, but from the entire nation. There were young children selling lemonade and iced tea in front of their houses. There were adults from all parts of our society collecting needed supplies. There was a renewed spirit of camaraderie, togetherness, patriotism, and concern for our neighbor.

There were so many unique stories of individuals who saw a need and tried to fill it and who saw a wound and tried to heal it. I remember reading about a man from

Port Washington, NY who made regular visits to the Family Center at Pier 94 in Manhattan. This was where family members of those who were still unaccounted for and presumed dead sought information concerning their loved ones. It was not a pleasant place. It was a place of grief and sorrow. So this man from Long Island would come down to the pier each day with his 4-year-old dog. He offered his dog to the grieving families to pet. He would walk his dog along the long lines of people waiting for answers, people anxious and wondering what had happened to their loved one. The dog's owner said, "My dog is not capable of evil, only love. If she can bring 15 seconds of love to people who are sick with grief, then we've done our job." Offering compassion, caring and love to those who need it: Is this what it means to be my brother's keeper?

When I lived in Chicago, I was a member of The Solheim Center at Moody Bible Institute. I played a lot of basketball there after work with a few friends of mine. One year we decided to form a winter basketball league where each of us would form our own teams. We realized we needed some direction and help with this. This was where Sean came into the picture.

Sean was the assistant athletic director at the Solheim Center. He helped us to use the game of basketball as a way of living out our life of faith. I'll never forget this one thing he shared with us which struck a chord with me. It was about what impact working together as a team can have. He taught us that when we play, each teammate should concentrate their efforts on making their teammates better players, setting them up for success, such as making the extra pass, setting a screen to allow a teammate to get an open look at the basket and working for the open shot. By doing so, in essence you inspire each teammate to play at a higher level helping them to become better players and build a stronger team. Sean said if each teammate plays the game with this in mind, then the entire team is able to play at a higher level and will enjoy greater success.

Dr. Martin Luther King Jr. in much of his writings and sermons describes it this way, "…All life is interrelated. We are caught in an inescapable network of mutuality; tied in a single garment of destiny. Whatever affects one directly, affects all indirectly. Strangely enough, I can never be what I ought to be until you are what you ought to be. And in the same way you can never be what you ought to be until I am what I ought to be." The truth is we are all connected through the common, interwoven cloth that is our humanity. Each of us is a child of God interconnected with one another. Therefore, whatever we say and do, we impact the world in ways large and small. Working together, building each other up, and putting the needs of others before our own: Is this what it means to be my brother's keeper?

The 9-11 tragedy changed our view of the world. It has led to U.S. engagement in two wars in Iraqi and in Afghanistan. With the rising number of hate crimes in the last couple of years and the political division and discord of our current time, I think it's safe to say that we face an uncertain future. I don't know what will happen now. We've got some difficult days ahead. But thanks be to God I am grateful. I am grateful for the hope that lives on in midst of division and strife. I am grateful for a faith that carries me along in my darkest hour. And I am grateful for a love that can overcome all the obstacles that the evil one places before me. Remember the words of William Cullen Bryant, "Truth crushed to earth shall rise again." We will rise again when we put our trust and faith in God and in one another working and living together in a spirit of brotherhood and sisterhood caring for one another. We will rise again when we partner together, united by such common goals as feeding the hungry, clothing the naked, and building homes for the homeless right here in New Braunfels. We will rise again when we live out the true calling that Almighty God placed upon our hearts to be a beacon of light in the darkness of night.

So am I my brother's keeper? The answer is no, no I'm not. I am my brother's brother. I am my brother's brother.

Let us pray. We are grateful people. We are grateful for the life you've given us, for the life you call us to live. Our gratitude pours out of us like water from a fountain. We are grateful for our gifts, our abilities, our family and friends, our community. We are also grateful for the call to serve in Jesus name; to be our brother's brother. Amen.

Boast-masters

Psalm 8; Romans 5:1-5

There is something I have to tell you today. I am awesome! I truly am. Ask anybody. They will tell you. I am the best!

There is no question that I am the most amazing person to ever live. Why you may ask? How is this possible? I know people. I know lots of people. Check out my *FaceBook* page! One thousand, one hundred and twenty-five friends. I am the best. I am popular and loved and respected and everything. Nobody holds a candle to me. I don't mean to brag. I don't mean to boast. But I am the host with the most from coast to coast! Simply put...I am awesome!

What does this sound like to you? Are they words from someone who is humble or someone who is full of themselves? Nobody likes a show-off. Seriously, nobody. You can probably picture such a person from your childhood or from work or your neighborhood or your church. Nobody expects it's the pastor, though. Regardless, such a person loves to talk about themselves, their achievements, their possessions, and all the famous people they know. You get the picture. It's boasting. They are boast-masters: someone who is overly proud of themselves and filled with self-satisfied talk about their skills and abilities and achievements.

Nowhere is this more evident today than on social media: FaceBook, Instagram, Twitter and others. Nobody posts anything about how bad things are going. Nobody posts picture of themselves without make-up or with their clothes tattered and torn. I have never seen a FaceBook post that read, "I am mediocre. I live a mediocre life. I am so average. Woo hoo". We share when loved ones die, but otherwise we only post the good things, our achievements, the cool stuff we do and selfies with some famous actor, musician or politician. Boasting about ourselves has become an art form on social media. This kind of boasting leaves us feeling hollow and empty; unfulfilled and isolated.

How can we overcome this? What **can** we boast about?

Early in Paul' letter to the church in Rome, Paul writes, "The one who is righteous will live by faith" (Romans 1:17). Behind that statement is the reality that all of us are sinners and are unable to bring about or make our own righteousness. There is nothing we can boast about. Boasting about ourselves is without merit because we are separated from God. But in that verse, Paul implies that we become right with God not by anything we can do — not by doing good deeds or living an exemplary life or through acts of penitence. No, rather we become righteous by putting our faith in Jesus Christ.

Theologians call that movement from a state of sin to a state of grace "justification," a word that comes from the ancient Roman law court. In that setting, the judge had the power, even when he knew the accused person was guilty as charged, to pronounce the defendant free and innocent anyway, thereby granting the person a declaration of innocence.

Paul uses the word in our text today: "Therefore, since we are justified by faith ..." (5:1).

When Paul used the word *justify*, however, he was not speaking about our standing before the law but our standing before God. And if we are at all thoughtful and sensitive about how we live our lives, then we can hardly escape concern about our relationship with God. It's the rare one of us who has absolutely no guilty feelings about something we have done or failed to do. Almost none of us get through life without getting involved in things from time to time that leave us feeling less than proud of ourselves. We look at certain moments in our lives and conclude, "I was thinking only of myself," or "I behaved badly there," or "I took advantage of that person and did him harm," or "I wouldn't want my whole life judged by my behavior in that situation," or even "I sinned." Our particular actions may or may not have been *legal* transgressions, but they have the weight at least of moral shortcomings. And they leave us feeling bad about ourselves and uneasy about being in the presence of the holy God.

To be justified before God is to be made righteous, to be made right with God. It is through the work of Jesus Christ who provides hope based on the love that comes through the Holy Spirit.

Since we have been set right with God through the death and resurrection of Jesus Christ and at peace with God through Christ, we may, in addition to having peace, have confidence in our hope for the future. And our present status in God's grace is such that we can even maintain that same confidence in the face of adversity. God's grace is so powerful that even things that work against such confidence and hope only serve to strengthen it. Since we know God's grace, we also know that such adversity in our lives brings out patience and that such patience shows we can meet the test of adversity. Meeting the test simply reinforces our hope in Christ. It is the hope grounded in the love of God.

We are all too familiar with suffering and disappointment. Do they not cause us to question the strength and validity of our faith? If we are honest with ourselves, we discover all too often that our faith is found wanting; that our faith is weak and full of holes like a slice of swiss cheese or the Dallas Cowboys defense. To whom do we turn in times of difficulty and perplexity, in times when personal examination leads us to the edge of despair?

I believe our text today, with its message of peace, grace, hope and confidence, helps us to move through the perplexing problems we face and to find the answer in a hope born of the assurance of God's love shown to us in Christ. The deliverance from death Christ received in his resurrection is the assurance of our certain deliverance by the same God, who will defeat our sin and death as well.

When we have hope in God, our hope cannot turn to dust and ashes. When we have hope in God, we meet our challenges head on and overcome them. When we have hope in God, hope cannot disappoint us. When we have hope in God, we are more than conquerors in the trials and tribulations of life. When are hope is grounded in the love of God, it can never be an illusion, for God is loving us with an everlasting love, which is backed by God's everlasting power.

It is a hope worth boasting about.

But She Persisted

Job 42:1-6, 10-17; Mark 10: 46-52

I.

The 1997 Ironman Triathlon Championships is one never to be forgotten. The featured women competitors were Sian (Sean) Welch and Wendy Ingraham.[1] Ingraham was an Ironman champion and the top-ranked female in the world. With only 9 miles left in the running leg of the 140.2-mile race, Ingraham's salt tablets fell out of her wristband. Already experiencing dehydration and muscle cramping, she quickly faded, falling back into 4th place, with Welch being the last to pass her. But Welch was in trouble too, as she was also out of fuel, cramping, and dangerously dehydrated. She had already repeatedly vomited during the bike stage two hours earlier.

Through pure mental will, Ingraham slowly closed the gap on an ailing Welch, with a breathtaking, and somewhat comical, final kick to the finish line. The courage involved gives me goosebumps every time I watch it. They rumbled and stumbled their way to the finish line eventually crawling on hand and knee to cross the finish line; a line so close yet so far away.

---

[1] Ironman Triathlon, March 21, 2007. *Sian Welch & Wendy Ingraham – The Crawl – 1997*. Retrieved from https://www.youtube.com/watch?v=MTn1v5TGK_w

"I'm a persistent person, especially when I get my mind set on something," Welch says. "[Husband] Greg says I'm like 'a dog with a bone.' That year was special—I thought I could win for the first time. Of course, it takes a perfect race, but nothing was going to stop me."[2]

Ingraham didn't see a DNF (did not finish) as an option either. "You can never give up the fight for pain—that is only temporary," she says. "I would not have known how to do the race any differently. It was the day that was given to me; it ended how it was supposed to."

II.

Like these amazing triathletes, Bartimaeus has persisted and persevered through many an obstacle. He, too, has a biological problem: he's blind. He has a relational problem: he depends on others for survival. He has an economic problem: he's dead broke. He might have all these problems, but the one problem he doesn't have is that he is not deaf. He hears the crowd coming his way and he overhears someone say the name, "Jesus". He has heard the stories about Jesus, how he healed people from all sorts of diseases. Maybe Jesus can do it for him, too. And he remembers something his daddy taught him a long time ago, an old saying if you will: "The squeaky wheel gets the grease."

---

[2] *"Recalled: A Dramatic Duel"*. Inside Triathlon, May/June, 2013. Retrieved from https://www.triathlete.com/2013/07/features/ recalled-a-dramatic-duel_80471

He has a reason for his squeaking. over the noise of the crowd when he yells, "Jesus, Son of David, have mercy on me!" He has a reason for his screaming.

Now the road traveled between Jericho and Jerusalem was a dangerous one. From Jericho to Jerusalem, you gradually climb through this arid land starting from sea level in Jericho to about 3000 feet above sea level in Jerusalem. I imagine it's a tough, New York City type crowd traveling this trade route; a little rough around the edges and in a big hurry to get where they are going. They scold Bartimaeus for bothering Jesus. The Bible says, "They sternly ordered him to be quiet." How rude! Did they not know about the miraculous healing of Jesus that included blind people? Remember the one in Bethsaida? Bartimaeus is certainly worthy of Jesus' attention and compassion.

There may be folks in the crowd who doubt the ability or the desire of Jesus to help this blind man. They all have their own reasons, priorities, anxieties, and desires that consume them from the inside out that leave them blind and deaf to Bartimaeus' plea.

But that squeaky wheel keeps on squeaking! Bartimaeus is not deterred by the negative voices squawking around. So much so he keeps squeaking, over and over again, crying out even louder and louder, "Jesus, Son of David, have mercy on me!" He keeps screaming and squeaking until he is heard. It works! Jesus stops along the side of the road, interrupting his final journey to Jerusalem, the one that will lead him to the cross, to perform the last miracle of healing recorded in the Gospel of Mark.[3]

"Your faith has made you well," Jesus says to Bartimaeus. This faith of his is a persistent belief that Jesus has the ability to make a difference in each of our lives and may just do it if he so chooses. It takes this kind of faith for wheels to keep on squeaking when other voices seek to drown them out. The voices come not only from around us, but also from within us. And they are powerful voices!

● "Who are you to think you deserve something from Jesus?"

● "With children imprisoned in tent cities and cancer remaining to be cured, you don't think **your** problems are all that significant, do you?"

● "Do you think you matter to anyone? Are you worthy of love and affection?

● "You will never amount to anything!"

We struggle to keep on squeaking on our own behalf and on the behalf of others wondering whether the grease we need, the grease of grace, justice and healing, will ever come. As the last healing story in Mark's Gospel, we know the struggle is not over. We must keep on squeaking!

---

[3] *Living by the Word* – October 28, 30th Sunday in Ordinary Time. The Christian Century. October 10, 2018 issue. P.18.

III.

There are so many needs in this world – so many other voices crying out that my faith and the intensity of my shouting sometimes wavers. When I hear about Catholic priests having molested young boys for decades on end, I struggle to keep on squeaking. When I hear about the mass murder of eleven of our Jewish brothers and sisters in their synagogue on their sabbath, I struggle to keep on squeaking. But when I hear the news about a caravan of Central American people traveling to our country on foot and receive wonderful hospitality and assistance from the Mexican people, my squeaking makes a comeback. When I listen to the stories of the families who participated in Family Promise now living and working on their own, my squeaking does not waver. It rejoices! It rejoices and praises the Lord!

IV.

The squeaky wheel gets the grease time and time again. I am sure many of you do as well, each of us lifting up our plea, longing for the day when our faith might bring wholeness to ourselves, to those we love and serve and to the world.

Fearless Followers

I Kings 19:1-4, 8-15a; Luke 8:26-39

It was Franklin Delano Roosevelt who said, "The only thing we have to fear is fear itself."

We all know what fear is. We experience it at all stages of life. For a child, it may be a fear of the dark. For an adult, it may be a fear of change. For me as a teenager, my greatest fear was rejection. This was particularly evident when it came to dating.

It all started in 7th grade. There was a girl in my class who made my palms sweat, my stomach churn and my throat dry. Her name was Carrie. I was crazy for her! She dominated my thoughts day and night. But I was so afraid to do anything about it. I was paralyzed by my fears. I had convinced myself that she would reject me.

In high school, it didn't go much better. I was crazy about this one girl Liz. Liz was in my homeroom. I saw her every day, but I never got past just some casual conversation. My friends kept pushing me to ask her out. I put it off for a long time, again because of the fear of getting rejected.

One day I finally grew a backbone and asked Liz out on a date. She seemed very surprised and told me she had to think about it. Think about it! Think about what? Later that day, I got a note from her. I tried to play it cool, but my palms were sweating, my stomach was churning, and my throat was dry. I opened the note and read those four words that every guy I know dreads to hear, "Let's just be friends."

Let's just be friends? Are you serious? My greatest fear had come to pass.

Looking back on this fear of mine, it seems so silly and trivial. But no matter what age we are, we all have fears. We all are afraid of something.

What is your deepest fear? Is it the fear of rejection by someone you love? Is it the fear your family is coming apart and you can't stop it? Is it the fear of losing your job or getting laid off or downsized? Is it the fear of sickness or disease and even the fear of dying?

It's easy to live in fear. We live in a world dominated by fear. Just watch one of the many 24/7 news channels or our local TV news. They love to tell us what we should be afraid of because they know it grabs our attention like nothing else. Our morbid curiosity gets the best of us whether it's news or a movie or causing a rubbernecking delay on I-35. Fear is a powerful thing.

Because he has done the Lord's bidding in killing all the prophets of Baal in chapter 18, Elijah is fearing for his life. He must flee from Queen Jezebel's death threat (1 Kings 19:1–3). He did God's bidding with the prophets of Baal, but this is no time to celebrate. Utterly discouraged by the limitations of his own resources, Elijah proposes that he be allowed to die. Elijah has had enough. He is a burned-out prophet. Elijah is pictured as a broken, disappointed man moping under a single broom tree. He's stressed out and depressed, for Elijah it's the stress of fear coupled with the stress brought on by victorious success, according to one commentator. He can only see the fearful side, the darkest side of the situation as he voices his ego-centered complaint to God.

Elijah is depressed and depressed persons cannot usually be talked out of their gloom. What can work sometimes is giving such individuals a sense of purpose, a goal to shoot for, a reason that will get them up every morning.

God calls to him to come out and stand before God. God simply will not permit Elijah to give up what God has called him to do. God's response comes, not in the form of words of encouragement, but in the form of nurture (vs. 4–9), God's own presence (vs. 11–13), and finally in the form of yet another summons to work (vs. 15–18). Elijah is re-equipped and re-encouraged to do Yahweh's will once again. He is directed to set in motion the series of events which will bring about the downfall of King Ahab and Queen Jezebel's family.

God does not want Elijah to follow in fear. God wants Elijah to be a fearless follower.

For the man possessed of demons, the arrival of Jesus Christ means freedom and the opportunity to serve. For those standing by, however, this man's freedom brings with it an economic threat. The loss of an entire herd of pigs was not perceived by everyone as liberating! Jesus' power to do good carries with it a threat to those who fear changing the status quo. The Gerasenes are terribly afraid; they are overcome with fear because of the threat Jesus poses to the economic stability and well-being of their economy. The power of God for good comes to their community and disturbs a way of life they had come to accept. One commentator said, "Even when it is for good, power that can neither be calculated nor managed is totally frightening". The Gerasene people are not praising God that a man from whom the demons had gone, sitting at the feet of Jesus, clothed and in his right mind, wanted to continue to be with Jesus. Even as one of their own is healed, the townspeople count the cost and find it too much to handle. The healed man has become a fearless follower of Jesus, despite the rejection of Jesus in his own town.

We read elsewhere in Scripture, in Philippi and Ephesus, first-hand stories from Paul about powerful economic forces that arrange themselves against the Good News out of fear and mistrust. And we see it happening today. Children and families in the streets without enough to eat, without a decent sanitary home to live in, without a decent school to learn in, without access to basic medical care facilities to recover in and treated by many as moochers and leeches on our social safety net. What is our fear?

Syndicated newspaper columnist Ann Landers was asked once if there was one dominant theme in the letters she receives. She said, "The one problem above all others seems to be fear. People are afraid of losing their health, their wealth and their loved ones. People are afraid of life itself."

The Good News for you and me is we do not need to live a life of fear when we place our faith and trust in God in Jesus Christ. Fear is not in control. God is. God is in charge. But our humanity gets in the way and causes us to doubt and question what Jesus has done. Our human condition reveals our sinful nature. It is

27

what Christ came to redeem in each of us; to set us free from fear and anxiety, to face our fears, head-on, and become fearless followers of Jesus.

I charge you today to be fearless followers of Jesus even in the face of opposition; even when you're hurt and tired; even when all hope seems lost; even when standing in the looming shadow of death; even when the ancient Israelite queen wants to kill you; even when the proverbial rug gets pulled out from under you; even when you are so stressed out you can't see clearly, think clearly, reason clearly or organize life neatly.

"Our deepest fear is not that we are inadequate. Our deepest fear is that we are powerful beyond measure. It is our light, not our darkness that most frightens us. We ask ourselves, 'Who am I to be brilliant, gorgeous, talented, fabulous?' Actually, who are you not to be? You are a child of God. You're playing small does not serve the world. There is nothing enlightened about shrinking so that other people won't feel insecure around you. We are all meant to shine, as children do. We were born to make manifest the glory of God that is within us. It's not just in some of us; it's in everyone. And as we let our own light shine, we unconsciously give other people permission to do the same. As we are liberated from our own fear, our presence automatically liberates others."[4]

I want you to know today that because of the love God has for you, God does not want you to follow Him in fear. God wants YOU to be a fearless follower!

---

[4] Marianne Williamson, *A Return to Love: Reflections on the Principles of "A Course in Miracles"*

Whether you are a regular person with nothing special to offer or a powerful prophet of God having a bad year or a demon-possessed outcast living in squalor, without human contact and interaction, you don't need to live a life of fear. Trust in Jesus and be redeemed by his grace. Be a fearless follower of Jesus and your life will never be the same.

The only thing we have to fear is God.

Get Ready 'Cause Here I Come
Matthew 25:1-13

Since I moved to Texas, I've learned a few things about the Lone Star state. I've learned that the phrase, "Bless your heart" isn't always a good thing. I've learned that when someone says they're "fixin'" to go or "fixin'" to preach, it doesn't mean something needs fixing. I've also learned about the 3 "F"s: Faith, Family and Football, especially football.

I most recently learned why the students of Texas A&M University stand the whole way through home football games. Back in 1922, the Aggies were having a great season. They were on their way to becoming champions of the Southwest Conference. In January, they went to Dallas for the Dixie Classic. A basketball player named E. King Gill went along to scout the game from the stands.

But the team was hit hard with injuries. By the end of the first half, the coach wasn't sure that he would have 11 healthy players to put on the field. He looked up in the stands and waved for E. King Gill to come down to the field.

There were no locker rooms, so the coach brought the guy down to the field and put a jersey on him right there. E. King Gill stood there throughout the second half as the 12th man, so that if they didn't have 11 men to put on the field, he would be ready to play. He stood there, the whole second half, saying, "Coach, if you need me, I'm ready to play." And ever since, the students at Texas A&M stand through the entire game. It's their way of saying, "Coach, if you need me, I'm ready to play."[5]

And I wonder if, during these days and times we find ourselves in, some of us will feel the Spirit of God moving within us so that we say, "Lord, if you need me, I'm ready to play."

The kingdom of God is for everyone who is prepared and ready to play. If we are to be effective, Christian stewards, we must be prepared for any and all opportunities that come our way. We must be at the ready.

Each of us have obligations and commitments for which we must prepare. Every week, I prepare the Order of Worship along with our choirmaster, so we are not just up here winging it every week. I also prepare a sermon every week. I don't just read the scripture and start rambling on about it (although some sermons may sound that way from time to time!) Children and youth prepare for tests in school and prepare papers as they gain new knowledge and understanding of the world around them. Police officers, fire fighters, doctors, nurses, lawyers, writers, journalists, accountants, teachers and any work that requires a particular skill set, go through a great deal of preparation and training in order to take on their

---

[5] Harris, David. "The 12th Man: How E. King Gill started Texas A&M's identity of teamwork and support". August 12, 2013. Retrieved from www.aggienation.com/history_traditions/ 12th_man/ the-th-man-how-e-king-gill-started-texas-a/article_3d5df82c-0394-11e3-95ab-001a4bcf887a.html

required responsibilities. Because we know, in the words of American writer Elbert Hubburd, the best preparation for good work tomorrow is to do good work today. In the words of the Boy Scout motto we must: "Be Prepared".

Jesus teaches us in the parable of the bridesmaids that we must be alert and ready at all times. Jesus uses the wedding traditions of the 1st century as his story for our parable. It is important to note that the weddings of the Jesus' day were very different from our weddings today. They lasted for more than a week; the couple did not go away on a honeymoon, but rather they stayed home and kept open house. They invited and admitted their family and closest friends. The couple was treated and even addressed as prince and princess. It was the best week of their lives! So not only did the foolish bridesmaids miss the wedding, but the whole week of festivities.

What sets the wise bridesmaids apart from the foolish ones? They are prepared and ready to play. The wise bridesmaids value and admire and respect the bridegroom so much they willingly adjust their behavior and expectations to be ready. They are women who have pure hearts, who cultivate goodness, who guard their speech and faithfully wait. To faithfully wait involves being prepared and ready, not planning and prediction. Matthew is making the point that stewards of Jesus are to be concerned about being ready when he returns, not predicting and planning when that might be.[6]

Faithful waiting prepares us for anything that might come our way, so we are ready to play and ready to offer our God-given gifts to the kingdom of God.

There was an energetic young man who worked as a clerk in a hardware store. Like many old- time hardware stores, the inventory included thousands of dollars' worth of items that were obsolete or seldom called for by customers. The young man was smart enough to know that a thriving business could not carry such an inventory and still show a healthy profit. He proposed a sale to get rid of the stuff. The owner was reluctant but finally agreed to let him set up a table in the middle of the store and try to sell off a few of the oldest items. Every product was priced at ten cents. The sale was a success and the young man got permission to run a second sale. It, too, went over just as well as the first. This gave the young clerk an idea. Why not open a store that would sell only nickel and dime items? He could run the store and his boss could supply the capital.

The young man's boss was not enthusiastic. "The plan will never work," he said, "because you can't find enough items to sell for a nickel and a dime." The young man was disappointed but eventually went

---

[6] Doug Scalise, "The importance of being prepared," from a sermon delivered at Brewster Baptist Church, July 15, 2012. brewsterbaptistchurch.org. Retrieved June 27, 2014.

ahead on his own and made a fortune out of the idea. His name: F.W. Woolworth.

Years later his old boss lamented, "As near as I can figure it, every word I used in turning Woolworth down has cost me about a million dollars!"

Author H. Jackson Browne Jr. once said, "Nothing is more expensive than a missed opportunity."

Effective stewards prepare for life's decisive moments. When opportunity knocks, stewards are prepared and ready to answer the door. The preparation we do today enables our gifts to be used by others tomorrow allowing us to spend our time and effort, not on frivolous things, but on significant ones.

Preparing starts when we call upon the Lord, coming to God in relationship, praying and seeking the Lord with all our heart. Our faith is not one more item on a "to do" list. Our faith forms our "to be AND to do" list. Throughout Matthew's gospel, Jesus teaches people about living and growing in relationship with God. Jesus stresses that being spiritually alive means not just knowing religious information or even saying we believe certain doctrines but doing what Jesus teaches regarding love for God and neighbor.

The biblical truth is this: God does the planning; we do the preparing. God plans, we prepare.

And we prepare ourselves by living expectantly and hopefully. It doesn't mean we withdraw from the world in our own Christian ghetto. It means we are to live hoping and expecting great things will happen by the grace of God. It means we are to make ourselves available to be servants of the Lord so God can work through us. Christian hope depends on trust; a trust that the God who created the world will continue to love the world with gentle providence, will continue the process of creation until the project is complete, and will continue to redeem and save the world by coming into it with love and grace, in Jesus Christ. Living in hope does not mean immunity to the harsh realities of history. It means living confidently and expectantly, trusting that the God of history continues to come into our lives with compassion, redemption and hope.[7]

Faithful action done today prepares us to weather the unexpected timing of God tomorrow, even as it prepares us for a heavenly wedding celebration, when Jesus and his people, the bridegroom and his beloved bride, are joyfully joined together in celebration forever.

Get ready. Keep awake. Pay attention. Be prepared, for Christ is coming and coming soon. Amen.

---

[7] John Buchanan. *Daily Feast: Meditations from Feasting on the Word – Year A*. (Louisville: Westminster John Knox, 2013) p. 532.

How to Find Strength in Our Weakness

2 Corinthians 4:5-12

Sometimes the beautiful and extraordinary are found in the plain and ordinary.

When Michael was a toddler, he received a special gift from my Dad: a wooden toy train with an engine, two cars and a caboose. It is a handsome piece of workmanship. It was made from different types of hardwood giving the toy train different shades and tints of brown. I called my dad to say thank you. He told me the story about this toy train. My dad and stepmom were at a rummage sale near their home. My dad spotted this toy train painted purple and blue and green. The paint was chipping off revealing the many colors from previous painting jobs. It was ugly and old, perhaps time for it to be trashed. But he bought it for a few bucks and brought it home. He began to strip the many different layers of paint covering the train. Stripping away the paint he noticed the different wood used to make it: cherry, mahogany and other put together with their varying wood grains. He stripped the paint, cleaned the wood and polyurethaned it. This beautiful and astounding wooden toy train was found underneath the ordinary and plain layers of paint applied over the years. Where most people saw an old, dilapidated wooden toy train long past its prime, my dad saw past all of that to the beautiful and extraordinary hiding beneath the surface.

There is power in the ordinary. Verse 7 says, "But we have this treasure in clay jars, so that it may be made clear that this extraordinary power belongs to God and does not come from us." Back in Paul's time, clay jars were the glass bottles and plastic containers of his time. If you visit an archeological site in the ancient parts of the world, one of the things you look for are shards of clay pottery. Pieces of pottery help archeologists determine the time period of that specific strata of earth. These clay jars were fragile. They shattered easily. They were the most durable storage containers available, but their fragility was its major weakness. You and I are clay jars. You and I are fragile. Bishop Desmond Tutu once said, "We are the light bulbs. Our job is to remain screwed in."[8] So God's Spirit will shine through us.

The treasure is the light of the knowledge of the glory of God seen in the face and in the person of Jesus Christ. (v.6) This treasure is the extraordinary power and strength of God. It's not to be taken lightly. It is found in our midst contained in weak clay jars, jars very vulnerable to damage and destruction. I read about a person whose apartment was burglarized. The place was completely ransacked in the process and several valuables were stolen. Fortunately, a few of the most precious items were left unscathed because they were hidden away in a small storage safe disguised as a book, hidden in a pile of other hardbound copies. The story went on to describe a list of suggestions for hiding

---

[8] Retrieved from https://www.homileticsonline.com/subscriber/illustration_search.asp?keywords=martin+luther+king&Search=7&imageField.x=10&imageField.y=12

precious items, including air vents, pantry items and cleaning supplies, an old vacuum cleaner and a hollowed-out head of lettuce.[9] Perhaps we could add clay jars to this list.

This treasure brings light and knowledge to the souls of those who are open to receive it. Jesus' ministry reminds us of the ways I am weak and the ways that I am strong. What Paul is describing here is a paradoxical relationship; one between strength and weakness that exists in each one of us. We continually give of ourselves, so the treasure we have in Christ grows stronger by the day. The Christian life we live is a series of paradoxes where our sinfulness is intermixed with the power and glory of God. It is the paradoxical expression of strength and weakness in the life of a disciple.

For example, Paul writes we are pressed in on every side but not hemmed in. There are all kinds of pressure on us. Pressure to meet deadlines at work. Pressure to be the perfect parent, with perfect children and a perfect spouse. Pressure from our family to meet certain expectations. Pressure to care for a spouse or loved one who is gravely ill. Pressure to be the person you feel everyone wants you to be although you know it's not who you really are. No matter what the pressure we face, with God we are always able to find a way out.

---

[9] Gregory Han, "7 secret spots to hide valuables at home," apartmenttherapy.com, October 9, 2016. Retrieved December 30, 2017.

There is always an escape route for our spirit into the spaciousness of God's embrace.

Paul also writes that we are perplexed, but not driven to despair. There are times when we don't know what to do. When Michael had his first seizure a few years back, I was terrified. I was in shock. I was perplexed. I remember freaking out at the 911 operator who told me exactly what to do. You may find yourself perplexed by current events and what's happening in our world. The rash of school shootings this year and in year's past has perplexed me in the sense that I feel helpless to do anything to deal with this epidemic of violence. I see those in power and those who are well-financed refuse to deal with this epidemic of hate, despair and hopelessness. It must stop, but what can be done? What do you do? We are reminded by Paul that in those times when we don't know what to do, as Christian disciples we always know something can be done through the awesome grace of God.

Another one is we are persecuted by people, but never abandoned by God. Right now there are 11,200 unaccompanied immigrant children here in the United States of America. What we are doing as a nation and as a so-called "Christian" nation at that is inhuman, unjust and contrary to the Gospel of Jesus Christ. I'm sorry, but I cannot, and I will not accept that this immigration policy of separating children from their parents increases and/or enhances a more secure border. It is inhumane and unlawful. It is not right! But those children and their parents are human beings just like you and me. They are abandoned, deserted and forsaken by the world, but I remind myself that God will never abandon his children. God will never leave any of us alone. Joan of Arc once said, "It is better to be alone with God. His friendship will not fail me, nor his counsel, nor his love. In his strength, I will dare and dare and dare until I die".

Finally, we read from Paul that we are knocked down, but we are never knocked out. By the power of Christ through the Holy Spirit, every time we get knocked down, we rise again. We may be beaten down by our circumstances, but we are never defeated. We may lose a battle, but with God we will win the war. We rise above on wings like eagles.

So how do we find strength in our weakness? How do we find the beautiful and extraordinary in the ordinary and plain?

We find strength, beauty and grace through our weakness by surrendering sinful selves continually to God. The German Dominican mystic Meister Eckhart (1260-1328) preached, "God is not found in the soul by adding anything, but by a process of subtraction." But in the capitalistic West, we think very differently. We all keep trying to climb higher up the ladder of success in any form. We've turned the gospel into a matter of addition instead of subtraction. All we can really do is get out of the way. The spiritual life is often more about unlearning than learning, letting go of illusions more than studying the Bible or the catechism.

The great Boulder Dam brought fertility to large areas of desert. Many workers lost their lives building this modern marvel. There is a tablet there that says,

"These died that the desert might rejoice and blossom as the rose".

Paul knew he could proclaim what he did with courage because he knew it was the spirit of God speaking through him to bring others to Christ. When you and I have the conviction that what is happening to us as ordinary clay jars is happening literally for Christ's sake, you and I can face anything that comes our way. Amen.

Knocked Down, But Not Out
Genesis 40:1-23; 2 Corinthians 12:1-10

It was one of those phone calls that you dread; the one that is not bound by the limits of conventional time. The one that usually comes late at night or first thing in the morning when you least expect it.

I remember it well. It was the summer of '85. My Pop-Pop woke up that morning at my Aunt's house at the shore unable to catch his breath. He was in the hospital in critical condition. We drove all night to arrive at my Aunt's early the next morning.

He was diagnosed with emphysema. I guess it was all those cigarettes he smoked since his youth. He had tried to quit numerous times, but this time it was for real.

For the next fourteen years my Pop-Pop struggled with this condition. His life changed a great deal. I remember the loud, painful coughing in our guest room during visits. He stopped playing golf altogether. He started to exercise at the rehab hospital three times a week per doctor's orders. These exercises kept him going and kept his spirit strong. It gave him a few more years with us.

Over those years his health slowly deteriorated. He eventually was on oxygen 24/7. He was so weak in the final months that he couldn't get out of bed without a lot of help. In the fall of '99 he went to be with the Lord. We were sad to see him go, but we were also relieved. He had suffered so much pain and hardship during those fourteen years with emphysema. It was the "thorn" in his flesh he could not brush off. He could have given up and given in to it years before. But he persevered for those many years without complaining despite his condition. He remained positive and upbeat through this struggle. He believes that he may have been knocked down, but he was not out.

In our scripture readings this morning we hear about two individuals who are knocked down, but not out. Joseph is wrongly imprisoned for a crime he did not commit involving the wife of an Egyptian official named Potiphar. She cried wolf, made false accusations against Joseph and he was thrown into prison. While in prison, God gives Joseph the ability to interpret the dreams of two fellow prisoners. They were Egyptian officials who lost favor with Pharaoh. After some time, the two officials, one the chief cupbearer for Pharaoh, were released. Joseph asked the cupbearer to advocate for him to Pharaoh for his release from prison. Unfortunately, he forgot all about Joseph and never mentioned him to Pharaoh.

Joseph was a forgotten man. He was stuck in prison with no hope for getting out. But God never forgot about him. God was with him. Joseph was knocked down, but not out.

The Apostle Paul writes a second letter to the people of the Corinth church. He writes that he will not boast of himself, although other leaders did. He will only boast in other people and of extraordinary circumstances. If he DOES boast of himself, he will boast of his weaknesses. He wishes to remain humble in the Lord.

Paul confesses that he's been given a "thorn" in the flesh to prevent him from becoming "too elated" and boastful of himself. Scholars have debated over what this "thorn" was exactly. It may have been migraine headaches, regular attacks of a malarial fever, a physical aliment that left him disfigured, or any number of things that would cause him pain, hardship and suffering day after day. Whatever the "thorn" was, it's purpose Paul believed was to keep him grounded in his faith and dependent on God for the strength and courage he needed. Paul says he prayed to God to take it away from him, but God answered that prayer as he answers so many prayers – he did not take the "thorn" away but gave Paul strength to bear it. That is how God works. If I pray for patience, does God give me patience or does he give me the opportunity to be patient. God does not spare us from our difficulties but makes us able to overcome them. This is what grace is all about.

God says, "My grace is sufficient for you, for power is made perfect in weakness." It is the grace of God that empowers Paul to overcome physical weariness from his travels and physical pain from whatever aliment he had. God's grace also gave him the strength to confront and stand firm against any opposition and able to face the slander and false judgments so many false teachers claimed.

Unless I've missed my guess, is there someone here today who has their own "thorn" they're wrestling with? Is there someone here today who's had the wind knocked out of your sails? Is there someone here today living a "life of quiet desperation", as Henry David Thoreau put it?

How many times have each of us found ourselves wide awake in the middle of a nightmare; overwhelmed by what's before us. And too often we try to deal with it ourselves, through our own strength and courage, and sooner or later come to realize this is an exercise in futility. We get in our own way and that's self-defeating. We don't allow the power of Christ to give us the strength we need.

In Galatians 2:20, Paul expresses our relationship with God this way, "I have been crucified with Christ; therefore it is no longer I who live, but Christ who lives in me." When we get ourselves out of our own way, we make room for the power and strength of Christ to live in us. Then the things we say and do in faith come from the risen Christ. "For when I am weak, then I am strong." When I humble myself and put my "self" aside, it allows for the strength of God to live through me. And he'll live through you, too.

This is the confidence we have as Christians; we have a confidence that when life knocks us down, we are not out; we are not forgotten. We have a God who claims us as his own children as we suffer with our Risen Lord. He doesn't take the difficulties away, but he gives us the confidence, strength and courage needed to conqueror them.

Former Surgeon General Dr. C. Everett Koop said, "We grow and mature spiritually through adversity – not when everything is going smoothly…in a time of adversity or trouble, the Christian has the opportunity to know God in a special and personal way."

Dr. Martin Luther King Jr. said, "The ultimate measure of someone is not where they stand in moments of comfort and convenience, but where they stand at times of challenge and controversy."[10]

God in Christ does not leave us to our suffering but gives us the means to persevere through it. As Dr. Koop and Dr. King described, God knows that the challenges, sufferings, and adversities of life force us to come to grips with who we are, including who we are in Christ.

So, what are you suffering through? What is the challenge before you? What tensions are brewing? A pending divorce? Lost a job? Bankruptcy? An extra-marital affair? Or coming to grips with the repressed memories of a less than perfect childhood?

On the journey we call life and faith, we all lose our way, but because of Christ's death and resurrection, we are confident we will get back up again to shine God's grace into the world. It's never too late to get back up again and to finish the race God has put before us.

Recall with me a major highlight of the 1992 Olympic Games in Barcelona. In Track and Field, Britain's Derek Redmond was going for gold in the 400-meters.

---

[10]Retrieved from
https://www.homileticsonline.com/subscriber/illustration_sear
ch.asp?keywords=martin+luther+king&Search=7&imageField.x
=10&imageField.y=12

He had the top qualifying time in the quarter finals. His dream was in sight as the gun sounded in the semifinals. He was running the race of his life. When suddenly he felt a sharp pain go up the back of his leg. He fell face first onto the track with a torn right hamstring.

Sports Illustrated recorded the dramatic event:

As the medical attendants were approaching, Redmond fought to his feet. "It was animal instinct," he would say later. He set out hopping, in a crazed attempt to finish the race. When he reached the stretch, a large man in a T-shirt came out of the stands, hurled aside a security guard and ran to Redmond, embracing him. It was his father, Jim Redmond. "You don't have to do this," he told his weeping son. "Yes, I do," said Derek. "Well, then," said Jim, "we're going to finish this together." Fighting off more security officers, with the son's head sometimes buried in his father's shoulder, they stayed in Derek's lane all the way to the end. When he crossed the finish line, the crowd rose and howled and wept. Derek didn't walk away with the gold medal, but he walked away with an incredible memory of a father who, when he saw his son in pain, left his seat in the stands to help him finish the race.[11]

This is the grace of God. We all get knocked down, but we're not out. God gives us the strength to bear it and deal with it. Joseph was forgotten for two years in

---

[11] Wagner, Kurt. *Revisiting the agony and resilience of Redmond's Barcelona race.* Sports Illustrated. July 13, 2012. Retrieved from https://www.si.com/olympics/2012/07/13/derek-redmond-2012-london-olympics

prison when he interprets one of Pharaoh's dreams and becomes one of his high-ranking officials. We all have a "thorn" in our flesh of some kind like the Apostle Paul. Such thorns humble us and remind us that with God's grace in our lives, whenever we are weak, it is God who makes us strong.

So, get up. Get up from wherever you find yourself, in whatever situation you are in. Get up from drowning in the pit of despair. Get up from wallowing in self-pity! Get up from feeling sorry for yourself! Get up, stand tall and stare down the memories that haunt you and the challenges you carry on your shoulders.

You've been knocked down, but you're not out of the race.

God hasn't given up on you. God wants to help you.

God wants to pick you up and help you cross the finish line.

For in the end we believe suffering produces endurance, endurance produces character, and character produces hope and hope does not disappoint us. (Romans 5:3-5)

Mrs. Helen Keller once said, "It's only through trial and suffering that the soul is strengthened, vision cleared, ambition inspired, and success achieved."

It's never too late to get back up again, for one day you will shine again.

Sharing the Light: Looking Back, Moving Forward

Psalm 65; 2 Timothy 4:6-8, 16-18

Today we begin a sermon series based on our Stewardship theme for the year: Sharing the Light!

If we, the New Braunfels Presbyterian Church, say we are a light in the city, what exactly does that mean? What does that look like? First off, to be a light in the city is to share the light of Christ with the world. Sharing the light is a biblical mandate. Jesus says in the Gospel of Matthew, "You are the light of the world...let your light shine before others, so that they may see your good works and give glory to your Father in heaven". (Matt. 5:14,16) To share the light with integrity, you need to be continually grounding yourself in who God created you to be and your identity in Christ. You need to know who you are and what God is calling you to do; you need to know what he wants to do in and through you for the Kingdom of God.

I believe to move forward you must first look back; or as reggae artist Ziggy Marley once said, "you don't know your past, you won't know your future." We all need to take an inventory of our lives and get our house in order. I believe this is true for individuals, companies, organizations, and churches. There was a couple I knew from church many years ago who looked back on their lives and realized they spent more money on a ski weekend than they gave to the church annually. They realized their talk didn't match their walk. To move forward, they did something about it and changed their perspective and practice.

The life of faith is very much a journey, a moving from place to place. In looking back over this journey, we begin to see where God has been at work in our lives and in our church. These steps, when carefully put together, show us where we've been and where we are headed. These steps are the milestones by which we measure how far we've traveled on our journey of faith and what we experienced along the way. Over time, change comes to us all and we must adapt and innovate, or we will simply fade away.

When I was in college, we had a huge gym for basketball and other indoor sports with permanent rows of seats on each side of the court. For a small Division III college, Memorial Hall could easily seat 4000 to 5000 people. Each side had three sets of stairs that ran from the floor to the very top row. My friends and I would run up and down these sets of stairs just for fun. A full set consisted of running up and down all six staircases. It was a great workout!

I hadn't thought about this in a long time, until I came across a certain web site dedicated to the sport of (wait for it) professional stair climbing! Holy Cow! Professional stair climbing: are you kidding me? Unbeknownst to me, there are stair climbing races held throughout the world in some of the tallest buildings in the world. It is described as one of the most grueling sports out there. According to the web site, "stair climbing burns about twice as many calories than any other sport or activity. Because it is a grueling sport, stair climbing requires less time to do the same intensity of a workout. For example, if you run 30 minutes per day, the same workout intensity could be achieved with 15 minutes of stair climbing." There was a race in Jacksonville, Florida a few years back where runners participated in a groundbreaking 24-hour endurance event where the climbers repeatedly scrambled up the Bank of America Tower's 42 floors. By the time they were finished, they had logged 123,480 steps and 5,880 floors -- the equivalent of scaling Mount Everest two and a half times. And the choir thinks walking up a few flights of stairs to the loft each week is tough!

Point is, running vertical can be tough, but it's also a great way for all of us to achieve good health, a sense of satisfaction and a stronger desire to keep moving on our journey of faith. *It can help us keep going in the race of life.*

You get the sense from reading Paul's letter to Timothy that he's climbed too many steps to count as he traveled all over the Roman world preaching the gospel of Jesus Christ. Paul had certainly had his own share of injuries from a myriad of beatings and imprisonments. But now, as he stands at the pinnacle of his life as an apostle, Paul looks back and realizes that the race was all worth it.

"I have fought the good fight," Paul writes. "I have finished the race; I have kept the faith. From now on there is reserved for me the crown of righteousness which the Lord will give me on that day, and not only to me but also to all who have longed for his appearing" (2 Timothy 4:7-8).

One way to take stock of our lives is to look back to our past; to the journey that led us to where we are today. We can see where we've failed and where we've succeeded. We can see the joyful times and the sad times. We can see where, when and how God has been involved in our lives. Reflection enables us to measure what kind of stewards we are with God's blessings.

For Paul, the race was always about focusing on Christ. In Philippians 3:14 Paul says: "I press on toward the goal for the prize of the heavenly call in Jesus Christ." To the Colossian Christians he writes, "So if you have been raised with Christ, seek the things that are above, where Christ is, seated at the right hand of God" (Colossians 3:1). Paul spent most of his life traveling long distances, but he was always looking toward a higher calling; a prize worth racing toward. Looking back, he has a clear view of every step he and God have traveled together. Indeed, it was the focus on the prize awaiting him at the top of those steps that kept him going, along with the constant steps of the Lord beside him, giving him "strength," rescuing him from "the lion's mouth," and saving him for "[God's] heavenly kingdom" (vv. 17-18).

As Paul looks back, he offers encouragement to the one who must look ahead: his young protégé Timothy. The text implies that Timothy will be the one to pick up the baton Paul is passing to him and continue the long journey of following Christ. He encourages Timothy to "continue in what you have learned and firmly believed" (3:14). There will be opposition from those who want to take the shortcut or the easy way (4:1-4) but, Paul says, "As for you, always be sober, endure suffering, do the work of an evangelist, carry out your ministry fully" (4:5).

In other words, he commands Timothy and each of us today to practice what we preach as we move forward in our journey with Christ. We must demonstrate through our actions to all whom we encounter what we confess with our lips. For any of us is to have any kind of credibility as a Christian, we must make certain our own house is in order. Do we say one thing and do another? Do we promise the sun, moon and the stars but it always falls through? Do we praise and worship God in Christ on Sundays but forget about him the rest of the week? Do we commit our finances to God and don't follow through? The most influential stewardship witness we can make is to be good stewards ourselves. Paul is encouraging Timothy to be a good steward of his leadership role; to use it wisely, to be a positive example of what it means to be a steward of God in Christ. We must say what we mean and mean what we say. We must live our faith every day of the week, not just on Sundays. We must meet our financial commitments to our church so trust can be forged, and confidence can be shaped in our relationship with God and one another.

When you get right down to it, shining the light of Christ through the world is not a one-time event, it's a way of life, of wanting to do our best for God, of giving our whole selves so we may finish well. That's the whole point! Some will finish faster and stronger than others, but everyone who undertakes a race does so to do their best. We know that stair climbing is becoming more popular because it's something anyone can do. In fact, tower running is never about racing directly against your opponent. All tower runners compete against themselves and the clock, doing their best to finish the race in their own best time. Following Jesus is about doing the best we can, too. It's not about comparing ourselves to others but encouraging each other to share the light of Christ following the road that has been laid out before us; to do our best in running the race to achieve the prize -- the eternal calling of God in Christ.

This is the Good News of Jesus Christ. Believe it and live it. Amen.

Ordinary Heroes
Luke 10: 1-11; 16-20

On January 13, 1982, Air Florida Flight 90 crashed after takeoff and fell into the icy waters of the Potomac River. Lenny Skutnik witnessed the whole thing. He stood with other spectators on the riverbank watching a woman who had survived the crash struggling to swim in the cold water. Skutnik plunged into the river and rescued her.

Mr. Skutnik had never taken a lifesaving course, but he saved the woman's life. He probably didn't use the proper form or technique when he swam to the woman's side, at least as professional swim instructors would teach it. He may not have followed the Red Cross Lifesaving Manual in the method he used to grab the woman and bring her to safety.

At that time, Mr. Skutnik was a general office worker. He had a wife and two children and lived in a rented town house. He became a national hero on that fateful day by risking his life to rescue that drowning woman.

Mr. Skutnik was invited to attend the 1982 State of the Union address by President Reagan. He was the first in what has become an annual tradition of notable people being invited to sit in the President's box at the State of the Union address. The press refers to the President's box as the "Heroes' Gallery".

Mr. Skutnik is still embarrassed when people call him a hero for doing what he did.

"I wasn't a hero," he said. "I was just someone who helped another human being. We're surrounded by heroes."

Heroes are ordinary people who do the extraordinary. Jesus calls seventy regular people, people like you and me, people like Mr. Skutnik, to be fearless followers, to make our perfect effort and do the extraordinary. Filled with spiritual power, the seventy travel in pairs to every place Jesus will visit to cure the sick and proclaim the Kingdom of God is near.

This is not a walk in the park! This is not going to be easy! Jesus says, "I am sending you out like lambs into the midst of wolves." He tells the seventy that they are in for the fight of their lives. They will be putting their lives on the line. They will be vulnerable to attack by those who do not welcome them and do not want to hear about the coming of God's reign.

And if it wasn't challenging enough, Jesus instructs them to not take anything with them. "Carry no purse, no bag, no sandals." They must travel light and depend on the hospitality of the strangers who take them in. In many ways, the "stuff" they would carry would hinder their efforts more than help in times of trouble. How easy it is to be weighed down by all the "stuff" we own. We can get so preoccupied with our "stuff" that we have little time, energy and resources to serve the needs of others. We can lose our focus on what's really important in life.

Their mission is of critical importance to both the towns who accept them and those who reject them. With the towns who accept them, the peace of God will come upon the townspeople. Their only resource is the powerful message: "The kingdom of God has come near to you. Repent and believe the Good News!" Theirs is a message of salvation: the coming of God's reign brings deliverance and hope to all people.

With the towns who do NOT accept them, they are to wipe the very dirt off their feet. They need to shake it off and move on. The seventy are to not waste their time and energy with those who reject them. They will receive the word of judgment from the Lord who will deal with them accordingly. The stakes are high for all involved. It's a matter of life-or-death.

Jesus is calling ordinary people to become fearless followers giving a perfect effort in order to do the extraordinary. For the seventy, it is the power of the spirit that gives them uncommon valor and courage to embark on a mission that seems unlikely to succeed.

Upon their return, the seventy report something remarkable, "Lord, in your name even the demons submit to us!" In Jesus' name, they have a power they never thought was possible. The ordinary virtue of following Jesus suddenly turns into extraordinary heroism.

Uncommon valor and courage become ordinary traits of those who respond to God's call. Heroes are those who walk in faith and proclaim the Good News in all times and situations; those who put their lives on the line in order that the whole world may hear the Gospel. Victory over illness and evil takes place when we as Christians live in the world with the peace and power of Jesus Christ. It's not something we were born with, but something bestowed upon us by Jesus who gives us strength "over all the power of the enemy." (v.19) Incredible stuff happens when we, the people of God step out in faith on a mission from God. They are ordinary heroes who change the world in Jesus' name.

The late Arthur Ashe said, "True heroism is remarkably sober, very undramatic. It is not the urge to surpass all others at whatever cost, but the urge to serve others at whatever cost."[12]

We celebrated the Fourth of July, Independence Day, this past Thursday. It is the day that commemorates "thousands of honorable people from more than two centuries ago who made tremendous sacrifices so that we would be able to enjoy the freedoms we have today."[13] Those men, women and children, among them our Founding Fathers, put their own lives on the line. Families lost husbands, fathers and sons who died on the battlefield fighting for freedom. The Founding Fathers were men of means and knew full well that by signing the Declaration of Independence they could lose everything they had. They were signing their death sentence. They were ordinary men who acted and did the extraordinary. That's why they are heroes.

---

[12] Retrieved from
https://www.homileticsonline.com/subscriber/illustration_sear ch.asp?keywords=Arthur%20Ashe
[13] Retrieved from
https://www.homileticsonline.com/subscriber/illustration_sear ch.asp?keywords=Wayne+Gretzky&Search=7&imageField.x=1 6&imageField.y=5

"Freedom has never been free, but from those brave souls of 1776 to those showing their "defiance" against terror today, Americans have always been willing to pay the necessary price. The freedom we enjoy today has been purchased not only with treasure, but with generations of blood, sweat and tears." (FoxNews.com, Booker Stallworth, June 30, 2006) They answered the call to serve their country; to honor their God; to take a stand to establish and protect the liberties we enjoy and cherish. They are our nation's heroes.

God is always looking for heroes who will accept the challenge to be fearless followers of Christ making their perfect effort to be his disciple; to proclaim the Good News with more than words but with actions that are concrete and clear. We can be God's heroes.

It was one of my heroes Teddy Roosevelt who wrote that a hero is "the man who is actually in the arena; whose face is marred by dust and sweat and blood; who strives valiantly, who errs and comes short again and again; who knows the great enthusiasms, the great devotions and spends himself in a worthy cause; who, at the best, knows in the end the triumph of high achievement; and who at the worst, at least fails while daring greatly, so that his place shall never be with those cold and timid souls who know neither victory or defeat." (*The Critic* by T. Roosevelt) This is the kind of hero God is looking for and will find right here among us.

Because we need heroes now more than ever, "to be lambs in the midst of wolves" (10:3); God needs ordinary people like Mr. Skutnik, like you and me, to take action and do the extraordinary: to feed the hungry, heal the sick, clothe the naked and to pour out the love and compassion of Christ into a world dominated by hatred and greed.

You and I can change the world. You don't have to be an expert in something or have an advanced academic degree or know someone famous. What we must have is valor, courage, gumption, patience, and determination to make the jump into the icy Potomac to help one in need. To do so we need to depend more on God's authority than on our human ability. We are to rejoice more in God's gift of grace than in worldly honors or recognition we receive; for we are God's heroes.

Which of us is willing to take a stand for the coming Kingdom of God? Who among us will put their lives on the line to take risks, to do the extraordinary work required to bring God's love, compassion, healing and hope into the world? This is our calling as Christians.

We are called to "strive valiantly…and dare greatly" to show the love and compassion of Jesus Christ to the whole world. We are called to leave our mark. What will your mark be?

Outplay, Outlast, Outdo
Genesis 32:22-31; Luke 18:1-8

Persistence pays off, does it not?

If at first you don't succeed, try and try again.

Hall of Fame hockey player Wayne Gretzky understood this. As the NHL's all-time leading scorer, he once shared the comment of an early coach who was frustrated with Wayne's lack of scoring. The coach told him, "You miss one hundred percent of the shots you never take." Persistence pays off.

Former Prime Minister of Great Britain Margaret Thatcher is quoted saying, "You may have to fight a battle more than once to win it." Persistence pays off.

I read an interview with a venture capitalist who said that he rarely sees a poorly presented business plan, less than five percent of the proposals his firm reviews ever receive investment capital. Of those five percent, less than one in ten meet their projections. This can be discouraging because it requires hard work, extra hours, research, follow-up – and still only one venture out of two hundred ever pays off. But, he says, when the one deal pays off, the rewards are enough to make all of the effort worth it. Persistence pays off literally.

Examples of persistence are found throughout the Bible. In our Old Testament reading from Genesis, we witness Jacob wrestling the angel of God in total darkness until the break of day. And despite this, he persists until the blessing of a new name and a new future are granted to him. Faith is about persistence and persistence pays off. In Psalm 121, the psalmist writes that our God is all-powerful and relentless in his pursuit of us, neither slumber nor sleep, watching our comings and goings guarding our days and nights. Our God is a persistent God, is he not?

In our Gospel reading, Jesus' discussion of the end times and coming judgment naturally raises the issue of trials we face, and the perseverance needed to face them. He illustrates his point with a parable about a widow who through perseverance receives justice from an uncaring, unjust judge.

We must keep in mind that in Jesus' day, in first century Palestine, widows were the most vulnerable and helpless members of society. They could not inherit their husband's property. There was no Social Security or Medicare, Medicaid or food stamps. They were left to fend for themselves whatever money, food and shelter they could find. She had no clout in the community. She didn't know the mayor of the city or any of the county commissioners who might pull strings for her to get her case on the docket with the judge. All she could do was to go back time and time again and hound the judge. She showed up regularly at the gates of the city where the judge held court and pursued him on the streets and in the shops. She would not let him rest until he granted her justice. She believes that good things will come to her one day. At first, the judge is indifferent to the widow's request, but then he is compelled to reconsider because of her persistence. She refuses to take "no" for an answer. He finally relents, saying to himself, "Though I don't fear God or care what people think, yet because this widow keeps bothering me, I will give her justice, so that she will not beat me down by her continual coming." Her persistence pays off.

But persistence, especially when it comes to prayer, is not easy. When Jesus tells this parable, he notes that the story is "about their need to pray always and not to lose heart." The widow serves as a reminder that in tough times and moments of despair. We are to be persistent in prayer. Prayer is not a last resort when all else fails, when all the best laid plans and programs and power plays have failed; prayer is the first and primary task of Christians. The widow's prayerful pursuit of justice became an expression of deep faith, the kind that Jesus seeks.

So what about the ruthless judge?

One of the primary tasks of a judge in Jesus' day was to see that the vulnerable people in society were protected, especially the widow, the orphan and the alien. They administered justice to those who need it most, to those in the community who were completely dependent on him. Although this judge knows his role as God's representative, he has a well-deserved and perhaps a well-earned reputation of being corrupt. He had no conscience and was resistant to shame. The only way he could be reached was by the peskiness of the widow, who refused to give him a moment's peace until he granted her justice.

When you stop and think for a moment, if this woman's persistence resulted in justice granted from an evil judge, how much more will our persistent prayers be answered by our loving, heavenly Father? Even the ruthless judge does the unexpected thing in response to a powerless widow and grants justice. God can be counted on to defend and uphold the oppressed. God will not turn a deaf ear to our prayers.

Sometimes it is not as easy as it looks. In her book *The Writing Life*, Annie Dillard tells of a skywriter named Rahm. She watched from the ground as he made soaring loops and barrel rolls and filled the sky with word-shaped clouds; he seemed the most carefree person in the world from her perspective. But when she later rode with him, she saw that in the air Rahm was not carefree at all, he was all business. He was totally focused as he concentrated intently on clicking switches and wrestling with the joystick as thrilled the crowds below. Persistence in prayer is more difficult than it looks, and Jesus knows how challenging it can be.

Remember what he prayed for in the Garden of Gethsemane? "In his anguish he prayed more earnestly, and his sweat became like great drops of blood falling down on the ground." (Luke 22:44) As stewards of God's blessings, it is important to recognize that Jesus' intent in this parable was all about persistence, persistence in faith, a trait for all God's stewards. It is easy to give emotionally, even impulsively, to causes that tug at our heartstrings. But like prayer, sustained, consistent systematic giving is a difficult path to follow and stick with, but one that we are all called to travel.

Prayer is hard work, although many people see prayer as a quick fix to solve our daily problems. How many of us have prayed at one time in our lives, "O Lord, let me find a parking space near the door of my office building." or "O God, protect my investment portfolio from the instability of the stock market." Or we may even try to bargain with God and pray, "O God, if you help me just this one time to get home safely, I promise I will go to church every Sunday for the rest of my life."

Prayer is a way of life. It's not a one-time, shot in the dark for a good laugh kind of experience. I know when I persist in prayer, I mean really persist, with clear eyes and a full heart over a long period of time, something happens to me. Prayer doesn't change God; it changes the one who prays. I find I'm a different person. I have a greater sense of who I am, to whom I belong and to what truly matters in life. My heart grows stronger. My heart becomes less fragile and more free. Prayer and stewardship are a way of life.

Jesus also knows how tempting it is to quit and give up, whether it's managing our God-given resources or our prayer life. Back to Jesus in Gethsemane, we hear Jesus's temptation revealed, "If it is possible, let this cup pass from me" (Matt. 26:39). When life gets tough and difficult, we are prone to succumb to the evil forces all around us, whether it's about praying or giving. When we are ready to give in and quit, offering heartfelt prayers to God takes the focus off of ourselves and our circumstances and shifts them squarely on God where they belong. For in the real world we recognize that persistence is the key to a full and fruitful faith.

Whether we are learning to play the piano or entering school as an adult, persistence is the key. Whether we are overcoming an addiction or digging out of financial debt, persistence is the key.

When I think about what persistence can do, I think about people like Thomas Edison. Did you know that Thomas Edison's teachers said he was "too stupid to learn anything?" He was fired from his first two jobs for being "non-productive." As an inventor, Edison made 1,000 unsuccessful attempts at inventing the light bulb. When a reporter asked, "How did it feel to fail 1,000 times?" Edison replied; I didn't fail 1,000 times. The light bulb was an invention with 1,000 steps." Persistence pays off.

When I think about what persistence can do, I think about the life of Abraham Lincoln. Here's a guy born into poverty and faced defeat throughout his life. He lost eight elections, twice failed in business, suffered a nervous breakdown and was bedridden for six months. He could have quit many times, but he didn't quit and became one of the greatest presidents our nation has ever known. Persistence pays off.

When I consider what persistence can do, the name of the Scottish Presbyterian Reformer John Knox comes to mind. John Knox constantly carried the burden for his native land on his heart. Night after night he prayed on the wooden floor of his hideout refuge from Queen Mary. When his wife pleaded with him to get some sleep, he answered, "How can I sleep when my land is not saved?" Knox would pray all night in agonizing tones, "Lord, give me Scotland or I die!" God shook

Scotland; God gave him Scotland. Faith is about persistence and persistence pays off.

For Jesus the point of this parable is not that persistent prayer promises any of us what we desire. Rather, it teaches us that prayer offsets apathy and indifference. Prayer is a continual and persistent hurling of petitions against long periods of silence. The life of prayer is asking, seeking, knocking and waiting, with trust sometimes fainting and sometimes growing angry. I've heard it said that until you have stood for years knocking at a locked door, with your knuckles bleeding, you do not really know what prayer is.

Last Sunday I issued a challenge to all of you, the 5 Minute Challenge. I asked all of you to commit yourself to at least 5 minutes of prayer every day, praying for our church, praying for our new Associate Pastor and her ministry and praying for the future of our church and God's vision for our congregation. I believe that persistent prayer offered through the body of Christ can move the hand of God to breathe new life into old bones, to reignite the flame of hope in a world of despair, to make a way where there was no way, to make possible what was once impossible. Jesus commands us to pray always and not to lose heart. Believe, trust and have confidence that our God hears our prayers and determines what the answer will be.

Persistence pays off. What more could we want? What more do we need?

Starting Small...Ending Big
I Samuel 15:34 – 16:13; Mark 4:26-34

All of us have heard of Bishop Desmond Tutu, but few of us know who Trevor Huddleston is. Yet without Trevor Huddleston there may have been no anti-apartheid leader named Tutu.

Asked by the BBC to identify the defining moment in his life, Desmond Tutu spoke of the day he and his mother were walking down the street. Tutu was nine years old. A tall white man dressed in a black suit came towards them. In the days of apartheid, when a black person and a white person met while walking on a footpath, the black person was expected to step into the gutter to allow the white person to pass and nod their head as a gesture of respect. But this day, before a young Tutu and his mother could step off the sidewalk the white man stepped off the sidewalk and, as my mother and I passed, tipped his hat in a gesture of respect to her!

The white man was Trevor Huddleston, an Anglican priest who was bitterly opposed to apartheid. It changed Tutu's life. When his mother told him that Trevor Huddleston had stepped off the sidewalk because he was a man of God Tutu found his calling. "When she told me that he was an Anglican priest I decided there and then that I wanted to be an Anglican priest too. And what is more, I wanted to be a man of God" said Tutu.

Huddleston later became a mentor to Desmond Tutu. His commitment to the equality of all human beings due to their creation in God's image was a key driver in Tutu's opposition to apartheid.[14]

Starting Small…Ending Big: That's how God works. Because God doesn't look upon the outward appearance, but upon the heart of a person. What's on the inside counts more than what's on the outside. From small things big things one day come.

Storytelling is one of the most basic practices common to all human communities. Stories connect us to one another, to our ancestors, to our world and to our God. Mark notes that when Jesus spoke to the crowds around him, he "spoke the word to them, as they were able to hear it; he did not speak to them except in parables" (v.33). Jesus knew that only parable power had the ability to make the Good News of the kingdom a potent reality for every listening ear.

There are in the parable of the mustard seed an image every Jew of the 1st century would recognize. A grain of mustard seed stood proverbially for the smallest possible thing. To have faith like a grain of mustard seed means the smallest conceivable amount of faith. That's all it takes.

The mustard seed is the smallest of all seeds that grows into large trees. The parable of the mustard seed is also about the mustard plant. Both the tiny seed and the

---

[14] This story has been widely reported including by Tutu himself in a 2003 interview with the BBC and in Tutu's Nobel Prize ceremony.

oversized shrub are unlikely representations of God's coming kingdom. Let's not try to make the mustard plant into something bigger and stronger than it is -- Jesus found it perfectly useful for bearing the image of the kingdom of God just as it was. After all, we don't use the tiny mustard seed as an image of strength but as a sign of faith -- faith that God can use the smallest and frailest, the fastest, the slowest, the strongest and the weakest to help bring in the kingdom.

We read in I Samuel this morning about the anointing of a new king. The reign of Saul as king was coming to an end. God sends Samuel to the house of Jesse the Bethlehemite. God was to choose one of his sons to be king. But which one? After all, kings are supposed to be strong and brave, able to take on any conflict or struggle that comes their way. A king must lead his people into war. So such a king must be tall, intimidating, agile, mobile, have a clear vision, smart and handsome. He's the star quarterback for the high school football team. He is who everybody wants to be. Samuel goes through all of Jesse's sons: Eliab, Abinadab, Shammah and the others. All physically fit, well trained, possible candidates for future kings. Each son has the right stuff.

What a surprise to learn that none of them, not one of them, was who God wanted. Each of them has what it takes. They have the qualifications. Each of them has good references and impeccable resumes. They each have personal trainers to get them in shape. But not one of them was chosen by God. God says, "…for the Lord does not see has humans see, they look on the outward appearance, but the Lord looks upon the heart" (1 Sam.16:7). He's an afterthought, the last person to be selected was not even there. He's tending to the sheep in the fields. The smallest of the small, ruddy, with eyes and handsome to boot! He is the one. He's the one God calls to redeem Israel and King David goes on to be the greatest king in the history of Israel.

God can use the smallest and frailest, the fastest, the slowest, the strongest and the weakest to help bring in the kingdom. Starting small, ending big. This is what I love about the anointing of David as king and the parables of the seed and the mustard seed: God uses every one of us for something important and vital for bringing about the kingdom of God. Therefore, we shall never be deterred by small beginnings. It may appear that at any given moment our impact is small; but if that small effect is repeated again and again and again, it will become something great.

The late Senator Robert F. Kennedy, speaking to a group of students in South Africa in 1966, said, "Each time a man stands up for an ideal, or acts to improve the lot of others, or strikes out against injustice, he sends forth a tiny ripple of hope, and crossing each other from a million different centers of energy and daring, those ripples build a current which can sweep down the mightiest walls of oppression and resistance."[15]

---

[15] Retrieved from
https://www.goodreads.com/author/quotes/98221.Robert_F
_Kennedy

Try placing drops of liquid dye into a large container of clean water. Drop by drop into clean water. At first it seems to have no effect at all, and the water does not seem to be colored in the least. Then quite suddenly the water begins to change to color; bit by bit the color deepens, until the whole container is colored. It is the repeated drops that produce this effect.

We often feel that for all that we can do, it is hardly worthwhile starting something new at all. We must remember that everything must have a beginning. Nations, churches, corporations, small businesses, community service groups: nothing emerges full grown. It is our duty to do all that we can; to stand up for what is right; to speak out against injustice; carpe deum, seize the day, strike out and find new ground. It starts with something as simple as volunteering for Vacation Bible School in a couple of weeks. It starts with giving of your time and money to the ministry of our church. It starts with turning to your neighbor sitting in your pew today and saying, "God loves you and so do I. Be at peace." It starts with volunteering to serve in our community, in our state, in our country and in our world.

It is the cumulative effect of all the small efforts that can in the end produce amazing results. Results that will bring justice and peace to the world. Amen.

Surviving Your Babylon
Jeremiah 29:1, 4-7; 2 Timothy 2:8-15

If I had been one of the Jewish exiles extracted against my will from my beloved Jerusalem and forced to live in Babylon, I am not sure I would have welcomed or appreciated Jeremiah's letter. I probably would still be waking up at night with nightmares fueled by memories of the Babylonian invasion and the long-forced march to a strange and foreign land. Those unforgettable images would haunt me night and day: the city's walls under siege, the screams of neighbors succumbing to the wrath of enemy soldiers, my eyes filling with tears as I and others march out of our devastated, fallen city, with a heavy emptiness expanding in my heart hiking mile after mile toward a place I detested with all my being.

These exiles are overcome with grief about losing everything they held dear: their temple, their homes, their way of life. They are now aliens in a strange land, with strange customs, laws and traditions. Their hope...gone. Their faith...gone. Everything is gone. They want to go back to the way things were, the way things used to be. They want to go home.

This is the audience Jeremiah is addressing in our text this morning. His message? The past is past. Live in the here and now. You are called to be faithful wherever you find yourself: no matter how easy or challenging it may be. Here's how to make it through these challenging times, to survive your Babylon.

Your Babylon is any situation or circumstances where you feel unsettled, you don't feel at home; it's where you feel lost, lonely and abandoned. You could be mourning the loss of a loved one: a parent, a spouse, a child, a baby. Mourning the loss of the good old days. You're anxious about the future. You're wrestling with an addiction, struggling to financially make ends meet, stuck in a moment you can't get out of, waiting for a sunny day to take the lingering clouds away. It's wherever you feel you're out of place, out of touch, out of sync, and merely just surviving, that's your Babylon.

Today's lesson consists of a portion of the first of two letters sent by the prophet Jeremiah from Jerusalem to the Israelite exiles in Babylon in about the year 594 B.C. Jeremiah's letter is addressed to "the remaining elders ... the priests, the prophets, and all the people" in exile in Babylon (v. 1).

Jeremiah's letter is intended to counter the unrealistic and potentially harmful counsel of false prophets. Jeremiah's advice to the exiles in order to survive their Babylon is to undertake all those mundane projects and activities — building houses, planting gardens, arranging marriages (among themselves, not with their captors, v. 6) — things that constitute a settled existence.

In other words, God tells the Israelites to stay put and get comfy. Do not resist the captivity you find yourself in for it will not end soon. Don't be afraid to make a new home in a strange, new land.

But we all know people who would find settling in a foreign land very difficult. They are never quite satisfied with their situation in life. At presbytery meetings I can hear laypeople say that if they just had a different pastor, their church would thrive. It is ironic that in pastor's groups some pastors imply that if they only had a better church, then their gifts and graces would shine. In both cases overactive imaginations avoid a truthful assessment of reality. All of us play the "if only" game: "If only I had gone to a different school...", "If only I made more money...", "If only I had chosen a different career path...", "If only I had not lost my temper and said what I said...", "If only I had done this, if only I had done that.", "If only I had a brain..." This game allows us to avoid dealing directly with our reality.

Where do you find yourself today? What is your Babylon?

We can't always choose the cards we have been dealt, but we can learn to play them. Like a flower that grows through a crack in the concrete, sometimes, in order to survive our Babylon, we have to make the best of our situations and bloom where we have been planted.

This is Jeremiah's radically practical and innovative message of survival. He told the Jews not to resist, resent or reject their circumstances. They are to embrace them, take advantage of them. There once were two farmers who badly needed rain, but only one of them prepared his fields to receive it. The other did nothing but wallow in self-pity and complain about the lack of rain. Which one of these farmers strived to survive his Babylon? To bloom where he was planted? God says through Jeremiah that we are where we are supposed to be for a reason that's part of a larger, divine plan. In the meantime, in order to survive your Babylon, you need to put the past behind you, trust in the living God, put down roots, become productive and be good stewards of the gifts and resources you have been blessed with.

In the 1995 film *Mr. Holland's Opus*, Glenn Holland, a musician and composer, takes a teaching job to pay the rent while, in his 'spare time', he can strive to achieve his true goal - composing one memorable piece of music to leave his mark on the world. Teaching was to be a side bar in his life with his primary focus on writing his symphony. He approaches his teaching job as temporary; as a way to make ends meet and support his family while pursuing his true interest. As Mr. Holland discovers 'Life is what happens to you while you're busy making other plans'. The joy of sharing his contagious passion for music with his students becomes his new definition of success through his 30-year teaching career. His students are his symphony; his mark on the world. To survive his Babylon, Mr. Holland learns to live in the here and now and bloom where he is planted. In the same way, God calls us as stewards and as his disciples to bloom where we are planted.

We miss much of the past, the good old days, but whining and pining about it will not make it reappear. Instead, Jeremiah challenges the Jews in captivity, and us today, that in order to survive our Babylon we must embrace the place where we find ourselves, and find ways to be faithful in our living, so that others might ask about our inspiration, our resolve and our trust, and thereby be drawn into a relationship with God.

And isn't that what we are called to do? Amen.

The Fragment In Between

Psalm 27:1, 4-9; Matthew 4:12-23

Have you ever been afraid of the dark? I remember I was as a kid. I didn't want to go to sleep, especially in my own bed. With the light off, my bedroom was really dark. I thought at the time that the thick darkness of my room made it easier for the monsters to sneak in and get me. Of course, there were the snakes living under my bed, too, that only came out in the dark. A night light helped to lessen the grip this fear had on me.

The dark is very scary. The nighttime has always held a certain level of creepiness and fear; it has always been associated with scary creatures, ghosts and horror stories. Some believe it is in the dark of night when evil spirits would emerge and haunt the lives of the living.

If you have ever had to navigate through a totally dark room, you know what a trying experience it can be. As you take one step at a time, you grope through the dark, carefully looking for a safe spot to step. You're bound to either stub your toe on the bed post, impale your foot on a Buzz Light Year doll left in the middle of the floor, or slam your head on a shelf of some kind as you trip over your child's Thomas Train set.

The dark is scary and uncertain because you simply can't see anything. You're blind. You can't see where you are going. Sometimes it can be so dark you can't even see your hand directly in front of your face. To be blind and living in the dark is a very frightening place to be.

I heard a story about a man in Ecuador who later became president of that country and his experience in prison. He was arrested for leading protests against the government. He was locked away in a small cell isolated from human contact with no light and no window. For over three days he sat in his cell in total darkness on the brink of going completely mad. On the fourth day, a man quietly came into his cell and began working on something in one of the dark corners. He didn't say anything. He crept out, closed the door and disappeared. A few minutes later a light began to blaze in that corner. Someone put their life on the line to connect electricity to the broken fixture. The prisoner knew he could make it through his imprisonment because he could see again. The light not only illuminated his space, but it also brought hope to his heart.

So many of us live in the darkness of an old jail cell, some in total darkness and don't even know it. We find ourselves trying to overcome the darkness with darkness; trying to pull ourselves out of our dark despair under our own strength rather than with the strength found in the light of God. It breaks my heart when confronted with a person who can't accept the fact someone they love is an abuser or hooked on internet pornography or worse. It hurts to watch intelligent, gifted people who cannot bring themselves to confront their own fears, addictions, and who they are called to be.

Everybody has secrets, things we just can't face on our own. Some folks spend their whole lives trying to keep them hidden and quiet; they carry them with them everywhere they go. Until one day they must cut it loose or let it pull them down deeper into darkness. Until one day they realize they must let it go and give it up to God otherwise these secrets will cause them to slip further and further into the bottomless abyss.[16]

Ask the recovering alcoholic or drug addict if they are recovering under their own power or a power beyond themselves. Ask anyone wrestling and struggling with depression where they find the strength they need to get up in the morning. Ask the parent with a disabled child at home how they keep going each day.

Throughout human history, we've witnessed revolutionaries oppressed by those in power over them, who want to fight against the oppression of their people, revolt against their oppressors through military force and take power. All too often, however, one oppressive government is overthrown and replaced by another equally oppressive government. They are fighting the darkness with darkness.

Even Jesus was pushed to launch some kind of movement to throw off the chains of Roman occupation that would sweep him into power, privilege and glory. They did not understand that Jesus was

---

[16] Adapted from the lyrics of "Darkness on the Edge of Town" Copyright © Bruce Springsteen (ASCAP) Columbia Records © 2009 Thrill Hill Productions, Inc. - Powered by Signatures Network

called to bring God's light into the world to overcome the darkness. And so are we. This is our mission. This is our witness to the world. Jesus declares, "Repent, for the kingdom of Heaven has come near." The light we seek after is God's presence in the world.

And this light creates possibilities for living that did not previously exist. Light does not merely illumine; it is a game-changer; it has cumulative and transformative power. When light is reflected into a dark place, what was once hidden is now exposed. What was once out of sight, out of mind, comes to the forefront.

Author Robert Fulghum told a story of one of his professors, a wise man whose name was Alexander Papaderos.

At the last session on the last morning of a two-week seminar on Greek culture, Dr. Papaderos turned and made the ritual gesture— "Are there any questions?"

Quiet quilted the room. These two weeks had generated enough questions for a lifetime, but for now, there was only silence.

"No questions?" Papaderos swept the room with his eyes.

So, I asked. "Dr. Papaderos, what is the meaning of life?"

The usual laughter followed, and people stirred to go.

Papaderos held up his hand, stilled the room and looked at me for a long time, asking with his eyes if I was serious and seeing from my eyes that I was.

"I will answer your question."

Taking his wallet out of his hip pocket, he fished into a leather billfold and brought out a very small round mirror, about the size of a quarter. And he said,

"When I was a small child, during the war, we were very poor and we lived in a remote village. One day, on the road, I found the broken pieces of a mirror. A German motorcycle had been wrecked in that place."

"I tried to find all the pieces and put them together, but it was not possible, so I kept only the largest piece; this one. And by scratching it on a stone, I made it round. I began to play with it as a toy and became fascinated by the fact that I could reflect light into dark places where the sun would never shine—in deep holes and crevices and dark closets. It became a game for me to get light into the most inaccessible places I could find."

"I kept the little mirror, and as I went about my growing up, I would take it out in idle moments and continue the challenge of the game. As I became a man, I grew to understand that this was not just a child's game but a metaphor for what I might do with my life. I came to understand that I am not the light or the source of the light. But light—truth, understanding, knowledge—is there, and it will only shine in many dark places if I reflect it."

"I am a fragment of a mirror whose whole design and shape I do not know. Nevertheless, with what I have I can reflect light into the dark places of this world—into the black places in the hearts of people—and change some things in some of them. Perhaps others may see and do likewise. This is what I am about. This is the meaning of life."

And then he took his small mirror and, holding it carefully, caught the bright rays of daylight streaming through the window and reflected them on my face and onto my hands folded on the desk.[17]

We are the fragment in between; we are the fragment in between God and the darkness, reflecting the light of God into the dark places and the lost hearts of people. We are the fragment in between calling others to follow Jesus and make them his disciples.

People living in darkness are assaulted by forces both known & unknown and they are mired in anguish and suffering. It is through the light of Christ all people can experience a new day, a new life filled with love, hope and grace. God has the power to defend and shield God's children from the things that oppress them. The light brings well-being and wholeness to everyone.

This is our mission: our task is to share a faith in Jesus Christ that is exciting and engaging enough to be

---

[17] (From *It Was on Fire When I Lay Down on It* by Robert Fulghum. Copyright 1988, 1989 by Robert Fulghum. Adapted by permission of Villard Books, a division of Random House, Inc.)

contagious. The message of God's reign is not for the tentative and indecisive, because it necessitates total allegiance; a complete commitment. It brings a severing of old relationships and securities that left us in the dark for far too long. It puts people in the position to follow Jesus. It places all of us in the position to repent and accept the new thing God is doing in the world with the arrival of the kingdom of heaven on earth. And when this happens, what was once impossible on our own becomes possible with God.

The Bible says, "if anyone is in Christ, there is a new creation. The old life is gone; a new life has begun." And so it is as the fragment in between reflecting the light of Christ into dark corners. Lives change. Perspectives change. New possibilities are more enticing and alluring. This causes successful fishermen to throw down their nets, leave their boats and families behind and follow Jesus. People who held prominent jobs and successful careers in law, medicine or business and where miserable and unsatisfied, suddenly find themselves called and drawn to ministry and serving in Jesus' name rather than their corporate insignia. I could have done many things with my life and most of them led to dark, dead-ends, but through the light of Christ this is what I am called to do.

It is light that revives and flourishes; it is in the light that one can see the way. Where the light of God is present, there distortions are straightened, falsehoods are exposed, lies are uncovered, demons are exorcised, the lame walk, the blind see: God's light brings God's rule. And God's rule means the exercise of God's

83

power to make things right, to make things whole again. Where the light meets the dark, this is where the healing begins. Where the light meets the dark, this is where the healing starts.[18]

Repent and hear the Good News! The Kingdom of Heaven has come near." Amen.

---

[18] "Healing Begins", Mike Donehey/Jason Ingram/Jeff Owen; © 2010 Sony/ATV Timber Publishing / West Main Music / Formerly Music / Windsor Hill Music (SESAC) / Sony/ATV Cross Keys Publishing / Mt. Roskill Music / Robots Rule the World (ASCAP)

Longing for Home
Zephaniah 3:14-20; Philippians 4:4-7

Once upon a time I wrote on my Facebook page the phrase: "Home is…" inviting anyone to complete the sentence. I wondered what kind of responses I would receive. I received some well-known sayings such as, "Home is where the heart is."; "Home is where you hang your hat."; "Home is the sailor, home from sea." I also received, "Home is where I am welcomed, loved and accepted as I am." "Home is where people go when they are tired of being nice." According to writer and poet Robert Frost, "Home is where you go, and they have to take you." But the one that caught my attention was, "Home is where your story begins."

Home is where your story begins. And that is where the story of the prophet Zephaniah begins, from his hometown, in the midst of the great corruption and injustice in Judah. We are in the 7th century B.C. around 630 B.C. The northern kingdom has fallen to the Assyrians. Judah has evolved into a decadent society, politically subservient and religiously corrupt. The people had turned away from God. The ancient faith of Judah was in serious danger of extinction. This is the context of Zephaniah's ministry.

The essential message Zephaniah brings is about judgment and hope. God's chosen people constantly abandoned their privileged relationship with God, like the Prodigal Son. They took God for granted, an example of the saying, "you don't know what you've got until it's gone". But now and then a passage crops up in which a restored relationship is celebrated between God and God's people.

The nostalgia of home is very popular this time of year as illustrated by the songs of the season such as "I'll be home for Christmas". There are also all those Hallmark Channel Christmas movies shown non-stop since Thanksgiving. The plot of many of them, if not all of them, is about a son or daughter who hasn't been home for Christmas in years for various reasons, mainly to just avoid their family. But the main character finally returns home to a perfectly decorated, well-to-do home in the suburbs and through a series of events comes to appreciate the home of their childhood realizing that all their fruitless searches in life led them astray. Home was what he had been longing for all along.

Pastor, author and teacher Frederick Buechner, in his book, "The Longing for Home", says home is "a very special place with very special attributes which make it clearly distinguishable from all other places."[19] The word home conjures up complex feelings about a place you feel, or did feel once, uniquely at home.[20] It's a place where you feel you belong and which to some degree belongs to you; a place where you spend the rest of your days searching, even if you are not aware you are searching or longing for home.

---

[19] Frederick Buechner "The Longing for Home". (San Francisco: Harper Collins Publishers, 1996) p.7.
[20] Ibid.

What does home look like to you? What does home mean?

Zephaniah offers us many different descriptions of what home is. Home is a place where you are "safe from enemies" (Zeph.3:15). It's a place of peace, security and safety. It's a retreat from the craziness of the world.

Home is a place where you are in the presence of loved ones, (Zeph.3:15) those you truly care about, who love you for who you are, who rejoice over you, a place filled with joy and singing. There is no better feeling in the world than when I get home at the end of the day and I hear three voices scream from across the room, "Daddy's home. Daddy's home" as Michael, Marissa and Meredith latch on to my legs. You know you are in the presence of those who love you.

Home is also a place where we live without fear (Zeph.3:15). It's a place where we can be ourselves. Spending countless summer days on the Jersey Shore was home to me my whole life, but perhaps yours is floating the Comal and Guadalupe Rivers or days swimming at Schlitterbahn, or even time spent with friends and family at Canyon Lake. These may not be our physical homes, but they are still places where we can sit back, put our feet up, and let our hair down.

When we have a guest at our home we will say, "Come on in. Make yourself at home". Home is for joyous celebrations of life's milestones and where we grow and learn and flourish as children of God.

Zephaniah reminds the Hebrews that in the midst of their joyful celebrations, God is rejoicing and exulting over them: as a father holding a homecoming party for the son who was lost but now is found (Luke 15:11-32), as a shepherd exuberantly calling out to friends and neighbors that the sheep lost from the flock has been recovered (Luke 15:3-7). In heaven the morning stars sing together again to laud this new creation (Job 38:7, Luke 15:7,10), and a great multitude of the heavenly hosts sings, "Hallelujah" (Revelation 19:6-8), while the sea roars out its approval, the hills sing together for joy, and the trees of the field clap their hands. The Book of Zephaniah starts with judgment from God and ends with almost unimaginable joy.[21]

We find so much joy at home. It could be home the school or home as Grandma's house or home the coffee shop. I think that's why when our home is robbed, we feel so violated, so exposed and so afraid. The place where we could live without fear gets spoiled.

And home has taken on a whole new meaning for families in San Bernardino, Colorado Springs, and Newtown, CT, who still struggle to make sense of the tragedy they experienced three years ago tomorrow. The shock and horror of these evil acts will be felt for generations to come. Homes and families destroyed; the serenity of quiet communities torn apart by the murdering of innocent people. The home these people once knew no longer exists.

---

[21] Elizabeth Achtemeier. "Nahum – Malachi" (Atlanta: John Knox Press, 1986) p.86.

The Good News is that the season of Advent, this time of waiting and preparing for the promised Messiah, is the time when we are reminded that even though horrible things are happening in the world, even though people continue to destroy one another, even though wars among nations and religions rage on, we are reminded, first and foremost, that God is with us. Emmanuel: God is with us. God celebrates with us and cries with us. God stands by us in times of grief and sorrow. God is with us.

When we confess Jesus as Lord, by the grace of God, we have it in us to be Christ to other people. We all have the life-giving, lifesaving, life-invigorating power to be Christ to others, and sometimes to ourselves. I believe, as Frederick Buechner does, that it is when this power is alive in me and through me that I come closest to being truly home. I cannot claim I have found the home I long for every day of my life, not by a long shot, but I believe in my heart I have found, and maybe had always known, the way that leads to it. I believe the home we long for and belong to is finally where Christ is. I believe our home is Christ's kingdom, which exists both within us and among us as we journey through the world in search of it.[22]

Home is where the Lord is. When we are with God, we are truly home. Amen.

---

[22] Frederick Buechner "The Longing for Home". (San Francisco: Harper Collins Publishers, 1996) p.7.

The Rising

Psalm 130; Mark 5:21-43

I.

It all started at an ordinary kitchen table; the place where families gather together for meals and holiday celebrations; a place where kids tell their parents about their day at school. It was from an ordinary kitchen table that a mother started a movement that would change the conscience of our nation.

On May 3, 1980, her daughter and friend were walking to a church carnival when a three- time repeat offender drunk driver hit the daughter from behind, sending her 125 feet through the air where she died. Her mother began a movement to change the drunk driving laws in California and later across the country. This movement is known as M.A.D.D.: Mothers' Against Drunk Driving. It is estimated that M.A.D.D. has saved over 330,000 lives since 1980.[23]

M.A.D.D. took on the status quo, challenging lawmakers to do more to prevent drunk driving. It was sparked by righteous discontent; it was an act of social defiance; it was a rebellious, resilient reach, similar to the reach made to Jesus by the hemorrhaging woman and by a leader of the synagogue, Jairus. Two very different people coming from two different positions in society looking for a change, looking for hope in their hopeless situations, looking for healing and wholeness they believe they would find in the person

---

[23] Retrieved from https://www.madd.org/about-us/our-story

of Jesus. There is something about Jesus that prompts them to appear in public, to make their rebellious, resilient reach to Jesus, in spite of the social and religious ramifications. One an outcast who is ceremonially unclean. The other a part of the power structure os his religion.

II.

It is Mark's writing style to intermix the stories of Jesus; to start with one story, break from it briefly for another, which then is completed before the former story resumes. The result is the ability to observe the subjects of both stories to see how they are the compare to one another.

First, both characters take the initiative in dealing with Jesus and both do so out of hopeless and desperate situation. Jairus' daughter is dying and like any caring, loving parent he doesn't want to lose her. Any of us here today can identify with the pain and panic at the prospect of losing a child. When your child hurts, you hurt. When you child cries, you cry. When your child laughs hysterically, you laugh right along with them. And you know he's desperate because he is a leader of the synagogue, and as its leader he goes outside his circle of power and influence for help. After all, the circumstances are dire, and Jesus is his only option if his daughter is going to live. The woman is also desperate. She has been hemorrhaging for twelve years unable to find a cure. It has made her sick and physically weak, but also spiritually unclean. Since she is unclean, she has been unable to live life like everyone else. She is isolated from mainstream Jewish life; an outcast living apart from her friends and family.

The second similarity is that both Jairus and the woman are confronted with pronouncements by the experts that their situations are beyond help. They say there is nothing more that can be done to stop the bleeding and bring the daughter back to life. The woman had been bleeding for twelve years and "...she had endured much under many physicians and had spent all that she had; and she was no better, but rather grew worse." (5:26) This demonstrates to us how serious her health issues were, but also to the ineffectiveness of the professional "doctors". Jairus is faced with the reality that his daughter is dead and those around him saying, "Why trouble the teacher any further?" (5:35) Imagine the side comments of those all around Jarius saying that he is unable to accept the "truth" of what really happened to his daughter. They scoffed and laughed at Jesus' optimistic diagnosis. What would have happened if they simply accepted the results of the doctors or the advice of his professional staff, there would have been no miracle.

The third similarity is, in spite of their circumstances, both the woman and Jairus come to Jesus in faith. Jairus' plea was genuine and straight forward. "Come and lay your hands on her, so that she may be made well, and live." (5:23) He's not asking for some elaborate ritual to be performed. He's not asking for Jesus to follow the teachings of the Torah to the letter of the law. Just touch her, Jesus, and she will be well and live. He has no doubt that Jesus can help. He has confidence in Jesus' touch to heal his daughter. Even upon learning that his daughter has died, Jesus says, "Do not fear, only believe". That is, don't stop believin'. Don't stop believin'. I think it is amazing to see the esteemed religious leader of a synagogue demonstrate such trust in another religious leader whom his fellow Jews were plotting to destroy.

The woman also comes to Jesus in faith believing that, "If I but touch his clothes, I will be made well." (5:28) Again nothing fancy. No hub bub. No glitz. No glamour. Just need to touch his clothes. It will take two seconds and then she's outta here. She doesn't settle for the prognosis of the physicians. She takes her illness to the Great Doctor, the Great Physician. When she comes forward and admits she touched his clothes, Jesus commends her for her faith. It's not just a physical healing, but a spiritual healing as well. It's an awakening from a deep slumber to the possibilities of a new existence. What is confirmed is shalom, a wholeness, a restoration of enormous proportions.

III.

What's cool about how Mark mixes these two stories together is this: Jesus is rushing off to Jairus' house, when every minute of delay could be the difference between life and death, stops to search for and converse with the unclean woman without a name. We learn that she is of no less importance to Jesus than the child of this prominent religious leader. We are reminded that we are children of God who have been at one time or another knocked down by life. All of us have found ourselves traveling a dark, desolate road, running on empty, searching for relief, for safety, for a place to rest, for someone who understands what we're going through.

There is no shame to admit that you've been knocked down. Maybe it's the death of a child or someone to whom you were very close. Maybe you can't lose weight despite doing everything you can to do so. Maybe it's your spouse who is chronically ill and you feel helpless to do anything about it. Maybe your spouse wants a divorce. Maybe your child suffers from addiction and they're in jail or rehab struggling to get clean.

Like yeast raises dough into bread, I believe you and I can rise above. Every person of faith who suffers, such as the hemorrhaging woman and the desperate parents of the dying little girl, prays for and usually believes in the possibility of God's miraculous healing. The poet William Cullen Bryant says, "Truth crushed to earth will rise again."

Jairus and the hemorrhaging woman challenge us to examine our own faith, asking how do we find the strength to claim God's promises of healing and hope for ourselves and how do we empower others to do the same.

But the rising of the people of God is not just for us. It's for all people. It's for those living on the margins of society; the homeless, the hungry, the disabled, the mentally ill, the imprisoned. And not only them, but also the refugee, the migrant, the countless confused, misused, abused, and strung out souls whose wounds cannot be nursed: all have a place at the table in the kingdom of God. May this serve as a reminder to all of us that with a faith like Jairus and the woman, God can change us and reorient us to live for him.

The Storm Is Passing Over
Psalm 9:9-20; Mark 4:35-41

We are not strangers to stormy weather.

Maria. Harvey. Irma. Sandy. Ike. Katrina. Andrew. Agnes: These are the names of some of the most devastating hurricanes in history -- storms whose impact on the lives of people continue long after the clouds have parted, the floods receded, and the winds died down.

We watched with horror the devastation wrought by Hurricane Harvey on the Gulf Coast in 2017. Interstates in Houston became surging rapids. Harvey was soon followed by Irma and Maria. Irma and Maria devastated many islands in the Caribbean like Puerto Rico, who lost most of their infrastructure. The recovery from these storms is ongoing and will take years but, even then, the memories will linger.

The fishermen of Galilee didn't put names to the many storms that came whirling out of the Valley of the Doves on the western shore of Lake Galilee. They weren't pagans, so they didn't believe that the forces of nature were some pagan god throwing a tantrum. As Jews, they believed in the one Creator God, but they also knew that these storms were a real threat to their lives and livelihoods. While they didn't give names to them, they knew that whenever a squall blew up on the lake, it was a reminder that they were still subject to the forces of chaos, evil and death.

In much of Scripture, the sea represents calamity and chaos. All we must do is turn back to the first verses of Genesis to see that the sea represents chaos. When God created the heavens and the earth, "the earth was a formless void and darkness covered the face of the deep, while a wind from God swept over the face of the waters" (Genesis 1:2). Darkness, wind, deep: the image of a churning storm. And yet, amid the stormy chaos, God begins to separate things out, bringing light to pierce the darkness, separating the waters and the waters from the land. The creation story is how God begins to bring order out of chaos, which becomes a metaphor for the whole biblical story: the story of how God deals with evil -- both natural and moral evil.

The chaos rages once again; rickety boats are swamped by 10-foot waves and are starting to sink. Fear, panic and desperation come over these fishermen, who have clearly never experienced this type of storm (vv. 35-37). Look at this.

This is an ancient wooden fishing boat found along the shores of Galilee. It was found buried deep in the

mud during a very dry season. The level of the lake dropped enough to find this boat encased in mud. It was carefully removed through a pain-staking process and is now on display covered in clear wax. The boat dates to sometime between 120 BCE to 40 AD, the period when Jesus walked the earth. This boat, or one like it, would have been used for fishing or to sail across the Sea of Galilee.

Mark tells us that amid all the chaos, Jesus is in the stern of the boat napping quietly on a cushion (v. 38). The disciples, meanwhile, are in a panic. Jesus apparently doesn't sense the chaos, the evil that surrounds them, and so they are concerned. "Wake up!" they yell over the howling wind. "Don't you see that we're dying here? Don't you care?" (v. 39 paraphrase).

Jesus wakes up, and maybe looks at them for a long moment with one eye open. He doesn't answer their question. Instead he stands and addresses the wind and the waves. Mark says that he "rebuked" the wind and said to the sea, "Peace! Be still!" (v. 39) Mark, as well as the other gospels, makes it clear: Jesus has command over the wind and waves, over chaos and calamity and over evil and despair. He is the ruler of all nature.

This story is used by Mark to nurture trust in Jesus Christ amid stress and persecution. The early church community is challenged by Jesus to trust in Him more and more. To have faith in Him always, even amid the storms when they feared for their lives and cried out in panic.

What storms are passing in your life? Of what are you most afraid? What peace do you seek?

Many devastating storms can hit our lives no matter where we live: Tropical Storm Divorce, Hurricane Cancer, Cyclone Childhood Illness, Tropical Storm Unemployment, Hurricane Extramarital Affair.

The storms of life hit us, often with great fury. And we cry out to God amid our storms, "Where are you, God? Don't you care that we're dying over here?" This is a natural human reaction to wonder whether there is a God, and if so, whether God is even aware of my problem.

Writer Shawn Craig, in an article in Christianity Today some years ago, wrote, "Obedience to God's will does not mean everything will go smoothly, that the wind will always be at our backs and that the journey will be easy. Jesus told his disciples to cross to the other side of the lake, even though he knew the wind would be working against them. Despite the wind's contrariness, they struggled on because they knew they were doing his will. The storm doesn't blow around their boat just because Jesus is on board. It hits them full force. Nowhere does Jesus promise his followers anything different."[24]

The Good News is Jesus is in our boat with his disciples, present with us and concerned for us even when we do not perceive God's care. To voyage with

---

[24] Retrieved from
https://www.christianitytoday.com/ct/1999/february8/9t2072.html

Jesus is to travel in peace even in a storm. We seek to be awakened to the possibilities of life lived in God's abiding love. All of us can have peace even in the most stressful, anxiety-provoking storms in our lives.

First, God gives us peace in storms of sorrow. When we lose a loved one, God is there. When we go through a major life change (spouse ill, transition from school to work, becoming a parent, etc.) When we experience a tragic loss of something or someone very important to us, God is there to give us peace and serenity.

Second, God gives us peace when life's problems involve us in a storm of doubt, tension and uncertainty. There are times when we stand at the crossroads of life and don't know which road to take. Tragically we don't humbly submit to Jesus' guidance. When we ask to know God's will and humbly submit to it, we find the peace promised to us. God gives us peace in the storms of anxiety in our lives.

Our God is like a Father whose hand will never let us go. God gives us a love that we can never escape. In the storms of our anxiety and fear, Jesus brings us the peace of the love of God. Like the disciples, we are rescued from fear and disorder and chaos.

A peaceful voyage is not the ticket Christians travel on. But a peace-filled journey, with Christ always present, is. Jesus Christ's promise is not to sail us around every storm but is to bring us through all storms -- still in one peace.

Am I My Brother's Keeper?

The Wounded Healer
1 Peter 2:18-25

In her book, *From Jerusalem to Irian Jaya,* author Ruth Tucker writes about Dr. Eleanor Chestnut. Dr. Chestnut arrived in China in 1893 with the support of the American Presbyterian mission board. She built a hospital, using her own money to buy bricks and mortar. The need for her services was so great, she performed surgery in her bathroom until the building was completed.

One operation involved the amputation of a common laborer's leg. Complications arose, and skin grafts were needed. A few days later, another doctor asked Dr. Chestnut why she was limping. "Oh, it's nothing," was her terse reply.

Finally, a nurse revealed that the skin graft for the patient came from Dr. Chestnut's own leg, taken with only local anesthetic.

Later during the Boxer Rebellion of 1905, Dr. Chestnut and four other missionaries were killed by a mob that stormed the hospital.

Dr. Chestnut sacrificed her own skin, her own health, her own life to share the love and grace of Jesus Christ by helping people in need.

Why would she go that far to help someone in need?

Dr. Chestnut's goal in life was not about seeking public favor and admiration or making lots of money and vacationing in the Hamptons, but rather seeking God's favor, God's purpose for her life. She was willing to forgo a comfortable, easy life for one with adventure and amazement.

We, too, have access to God's favor because of the self-sacrifice of Jesus; it serves as an example on how to live life by God's will. It's a message for all ages now and for future generations to come. It's a life of courage, suffering and sacrifice that broaden and expand our hearts and minds and we are drawn closer to God.

The Apostle Peter is writing to the many churches established in the provinces of Asia Minor, modern day Turkey. The issue at hand is the social tensions and sufferings caused by the conversion of so many Gentiles in Greco-Roman culture to Christianity. The Roman Empire considered Christianity at this time a foreign religion that was not welcomed. Many who converted were ostracized from their own families. To believe in and follow Jesus was seen as a threat to the patriarchal hierarchy of Roman culture; that it caused immorality, insubordination within the household and treason against the state.

1 Peter counteracts these expectations. He emphasizes that those converted are to imitate Christ by doing good and not retaliating against those who harm or slander their community. By his wounds you have been healed and have returned like lost sheep to the shepherd and guardian of your souls living in God' favor and promise.

And this kind of living is not easy; it doesn't just fall into your lap without any effort, discipline or sacrifice. Too many of us in our world are afraid to live a full and abundant life. There are too many of us who rather play it safe then take a risk.

There was once a young man who saw that love made strenuous demands on the lovers. He saw that love required sacrifice and self-denial. He saw that love produced arguments, jealousy, and sorrow. And so he decided that love cost too much; deciding not to diminish their life with love.

He saw people strive for distant and hazy goals. He saw men and women strive for success and high ideals. He saw that the striving was often mixed with disappointment. He saw strong and committed men fail, and he saw weak, undeserving men succeed. He saw that striving sometimes forced people into pettiness and greed. He decided that it cost too much. He decided not to soil his life with striving.

He saw people serving others. He saw people give money to the poor and helpless. He saw that the more they served, the faster the need grew. He saw ungrateful receivers turn on their serving friends. He decided not to soil his life with serving.

When he died, he walked up to God and presented his life to him—undiminished, unmarred, unsoiled. The man was clean and untouched by the filth of the world, and he presented himself to God proudly saying, "Here is my life!"

And God said, "Life? What life?"

God doesn't want us to insulate ourselves from the pain and suffering of the world. When we love others, serve others, and strive to be all that God wants us to be, we get dirty, we get hurt, we get used. But those are the battle scars that God wants to see when we face him someday. God wants us to get in the game and get our uniforms dirty. That's what Jesus did when he came into the world. He's our example to live by; to model our lives after because he didn't choose to play it safe; neither should we. "To this you were called, because Christ suffered for you, leaving you an example, that you should follow in his steps" (I Peter 2:21).

Courage, suffering and sacrifice of Jesus Christ is our prime example on how to live a life in God's favor. It's a life filled with amazement Mother Teresa once said, "I have found the paradox that if I love until it hurts, then there is no more hurt, but only more love."[25]

Human muscles, in order to get stronger and healthier, need to be worked and pushed hard to actually break down the muscle fibers. Only then can the muscle grow and become stronger and stronger. You have to lose some muscle mass before you begin to build up your muscles.

Martin Luther King Jr. and many civil rights supporters practiced non-violent resistance. They wanted to end segregation in the public sphere. Rosa Parks refused to move to the back of the bus where African Americans

---

[25] https://www.homileticsonline.com/subscriber/illustration search.asp?keywords=John+Wayne&Search=7&imageField.x=0 &imageField.y=0

in the south were to sit. African Americans ate at separate lunch counters and had to get their food from the back door of a restaurant. Martin Luther King Jr. became the leader of this movement and their protests were met with police attack dogs, bully clubs and tear gas. Our human tendency is to retaliate with violence; to return evil for evil. It would be easy for them to counter violence with violence, but they chose to react differently in a non-violent way. As protesters were attacked by police dogs, beaten with bully clubs and knocked down by fire hoses, they did not retaliate with violence against their oppressors. They took the beatings and the punishment even time in a jail cell preferring to patiently endure and suffer through the struggle rather than retaliate in the face of unfair suffering. It takes great courage to stand up amidst violent opposition and not return fire with fire.

Let's not kid ourselves. We do not want suffering; we want success. We identify not with those who are low and hurt but with those who are high and healthy. We don't like lepers or losers very well; we prefer climbers and comers. For Christians, the temptation to be conformed to this world is desperately sweet and strong. Yet, as the Apostle Peter puts it,

The legendary actor John Wayne said, "Courage is being scared to death but saddling up anyway." Christ is our example on how to live a life filled with abundance and blessing and gives us the courage to do so.

During World War II, a large British military force on the European continent, along with some English citizens and diplomats, retreated to the French coastal port of Dunkirk. With its back against the English Channel, the British army faced a German army that threatened to drive it into the sea. To save what he could of his army, British prime minister Winston Churchill called for all available sea vessels, whether large or small, to evacuate the soldiers and civilians from the besieged French beaches and bring them back across the Channel to safety.

An incredible array of ships and boats raced to the rescue—fishing boats and cruise ships alike. As the flotilla made its way to the beach to pick up soldiers and then move out again, Nazi aircraft set upon them like vultures while German artillery pummeled them with shells. Ships were strafed with machine gun fire, and some were blown out of the water altogether.

Three German fighter planes attacked the defenseless *Lancastria*, a converted cruise liner, whose decks and hold were packed with soldiers. One bomb dropped directly down the ship's smokestack, tearing a huge gap in her lower hull. Nearly 200 men were trapped in the forward hold of the now severely listing ship. No one doubted that the cruise liner was going down. The chaos, smoke, oil, fire, and blood, mixed with terrified cries of the men trapped below, created pandemonium on deck as those hopeful of surviving searched for lifeboats or simply leaped into the water.

Moving through the middle of this living nightmare, a young Navy chaplain quietly worked his way to the edge of the hold and peered in at the darkness below.

Then, knowing he could never get out, he lowered himself in.

Survivors later told how the only thing that gave them courage to survive until passing ships could rescue them was hearing the strong, brave voices of the men in the hold singing hymns as the ship finally rolled over and went to the bottom.

This true story testifies to the courage and compassion of one faithful Christian who gave his life to provide comfort, courage, and hope to the suffering of those trapped on that ship.

We are also called to demonstrate that kind of love in our lost and dying world sharing the amazing love of God with those facing hardships and difficulties. We are called to live a life of courage, suffering and sacrifice that broadens our hearts and minds and draws us closer to God.

May you have the courage to be willing to suffer and sacrifice your life in the name of Christ as Dr. Chestnut did for the people of China. May you be willing and able to get in the game. Don't be afraid to get your uniform dirty. God wants us to model our lives after Christ because Christ didn't choose to play it safe; he took a chance, remained obedient even in death and came out on top, the victor. Amen.

What Are You Looking For?

John 1: 35-51

I.

Another tutoring session came to an end. My student, Alvin, a 6th grade boy who lived in the Cabrini-Green housing project, finished his homework early. In the remaining time, we started to play Scrabble Junior. Well, we didn't get very far before it was time to go.

So we hurried upstairs and out the side entrance of the church. The yellow school bus was waiting at the curb with a mob of kids pushing and shoving each other to get aboard. As I went to say good-bye, Alvin turned to me, gave me a big hug, and said; "I'll see ya next week."

After the bus pulled away, I went for a walk. I walked down the street for many, many blocks popping in and out of stores here and there. I started feeling cold so I found a bookstore in which I could browse and get warm.

And as I glanced at the titles on the shelves, one book caught my attention. It was entitled, "What Are You Looking For?". I don't remember the author. What a funny title for a book! What are you looking for? What a ridiculous question! Hmmm… what AM I looking for? The question echoed over and over in my head. This simple question struck a chord in me. It resonated with me. Maybe it wasn't such a ridiculous question after all.

And as I left the store and re-enter the dark, clear, and cold night, I heard that question ringing through my head: What are you looking for? What are you looking for?

It echoed in my mind as I walked up the street past all the fancy buildings and expensive stores. As I walked, I saw the towering high rises jet upward into the night sky. I went by some expensive stores like Brooks Brothers and The North Face store thinking, "I need a new suit!" and "I need a new fleece jacket." While I walked amongst all this materialism and wealth, I came up to my church where I had been tutoring Alvin just hours before. I passed by the courtyard and the offices and proceeded to the front doors of the sanctuary.

I began to reflect upon my life and upon who I was. I came to terms with the fact that I had a job I didn't like. Even with my good friends and the opportunity to tutor my young friend Alvin, I still felt empty inside. There was still something missing. I realized I still hadn't found what I was looking for in life. It reminded me of a song by the band U2. "I've climbed highest mountain; I've run through the field only to be with you...But I still haven't found what I'm looking for." I was reflecting and thinking about all this, I found myself standing before the mighty, wooden doors of my church with awe and wonder, with fear and trembling and not just because it was cold. The question, "What are you looking for?" was now ringing in my heart.

II.

When Jesus turned and confronted John the Baptist's two disciples as they began following him, they were startled by his question and his confrontive style. "What are you looking for?" Jesus asked. Jesus is a straight shooter. He's on point: no parable, no gentle discipling. More an interrogation than anything else. During the course of Jesus' ministry, it would become quite clear just what some of his so-called "followers" were looking for.

For example, as his reputation spread, there were the throngs of people that crowded around him with various diseases and ailments. They were looking for healing.

- As his popularity spread, there were the religious authorities who began to question his theology and orthodoxy. They were looking for a fight.

- As his miracles increased, there were the crowds of hangers-on, just there for the show. They were looking for entertainment.

- As his wisdom spread, there were seekers like the rich young ruler who tried to second-guess his meanings. They were looking for an easy way into heaven.

- As his fame circulated, and his famine-quenching powers became the talk of the town, there were lots of people with needs and wants who followed in his wake. They were looking for the loaves and fishes.

When Jesus went off by himself to the mountains and was lost in prayer, his own disciples came and interrupted him, declaring, "Jesus, we've been looking all over for you. Everyone is looking for you!"

The disciples were right. Everyone is looking for Jesus, for the living spirit of God in their lives – whether they know it or not. Collections of "Jesus junk" (key chains, shirts, mugs, etc.) won't fill the void; bags of crystals won't answer the need. A safe full of cash won't fill the empty space in your soul. The answer to Jesus' soul-searching question, "What are you looking for?", can't be brought home from the shopping mall. Each one of us has a hole in our heart that only Christ can fill.

Jesus knew there were a lot of wrong reasons as well as wrong ways for spiritual searches. Our world abounds today, as then, with counterfeit Christs. When Jesus confronted these two would-be disciples with his haunting question, "What are you looking for?", the answer he received may sound strange to us, but it was actually a pretty good start.

"Rabbi," they replied, "where are you staying?" "Teacher," they were saying, "let us join with you and be your students." When Jesus responds to this address and request, his answer is an invitation, "Come and see."

Discovering the spirit of God, the presence of Christ, in your life is rarely experienced as a blinding light or a burning bush. Growing your soul, filling your spirit with the right nutrients and nourishment, is a lifelong process. The Bible testifies to at least four different shapes and sizes of conversions:

1. gradual conversions - John
2. crisis conversions - Paul
3. series of crises followed by a conversion -Peter
4. a crisis conversion at the end of a gradual process -
     the Ethiopian eunuch

As I was standing before the mighty, wooden doors of my church on that cold night, what was I looking for? I realized that night my conversion to becoming a disciple of Christ was not a single moment of clarity, but rather a series of moments, both good and bad, followed by a conversion, a transformation. I found Jesus. He was who I was looking for. I had known him once before as a child and a teenager. But that night, I wanted to meet Jesus again as if I was meeting him for the first time.

This culture is looking for something - desperately. They look for it in celebrities, elected government officials, stores and the internet, pornography, drugs, alcohol and more. There is a quest for some sort of awakening, a deep hunger for spiritual renewal, lurking behind all the scheduled chaos that fills postmodern life. Not all recognize they are even searching for something more to add to their lives. But there are a few who have become so consumed by their spiritual needs they have "dropped out" for the rest of their lives. For most others, pressed for time but hopeful to find "filling" for this gnawing emptiness deep inside the soul, the spiritual search erupts at odd moments and in peculiar ways.

III.

So what are you looking for? Is it making a lot of money? Driving a fancy, luxury car? Living in a large house on the good side of town? There are good people, well-intentioned people who do all these things and more believing it will lead to fulfillment and happiness.

All of us, at one time or another have sought material things in an attempt to make our lives whole. And time and time again, these attempts have been futile. They have all been in vain.

Which one are you?

Sometimes it takes long years of sitting at the Rabbi's feet, listening to his teachings, before we can truly claim our discipleship, before we can kneel at the foot of the cross. I had heard somewhere that we all must first ask, "Teacher, teach us," before we can confess, "Jesus, save us."

Is that, perhaps, the reason you came to church today? To continue your spiritual search? To attend your lifetime mission of growing your soul? One day when Jesus finally asks you by name, "What are you looking for?", you can give the only answer that satisfies: "Jesus, the Lamb of God." Amen.

.

Your Perfect Effort
2 Kings 2:1-14; Luke 9:51-62

A pastor friend told me the heartbreaking story of a young woman in his church. Several years earlier she wanted the lead in a school play, but the directors chose another girl instead. The directors did offer her a subordinate, although substantial, role in the play. However, their decision wounded her pride. She refused to take part in any way whatsoever. Her mother pleaded with her, but she stood by her decision tenaciously. Later the young woman told her pastor that it was the biggest mistake she had ever made. She said, "Because of my stubbornness and failure to admit I had made a mistake, I spent the whole spring semester of my senior year isolated from my best friends. While they had fun rehearsing, I sat in my room and pouted. The funny thing was that the play was great. Worse than that, I am not sure anyone missed me, but I know that I sure missed them. I learned a painful lesson the hard way." This young woman demonstrates that when we fail to participate, we devalue our gifts. We can squander God's gifts by misusing them or even not using them at all. When we fail to meet our obligations of Christian Stewards, we are the ones that are weakened in our calling as Christians.

How can we change this situation? What can we do to strengthen our faith and get back in the game?

Jesus and his disciples were traveling from Galilee to Jerusalem. As the day drew to a close, he sent messengers ahead of them to secure a place to stay for the night. The messengers came to a Samaritan town that did not welcome these two strangers into their midst. James and John hear the news of rejection and they are ready for a fight. They want to take the fight to those Samaritans. James and John sound like a couple of gangsters offended by the lack of respect shown to them and Jesus. They want to take them out, send this town of complete strangers up in flames and vanish from the earth. I can hear Jesus rebuking them saying, "Are you crazy? What's wrong with you guys?" In fact, in your Bible you will find a footnote based on some ancient authorities where Jesus says, "I'm not here to destroy human beings, but to save them from themselves." They continue down the road to Jerusalem where Jesus meets three different anonymous individuals; a bunch of disciple wanna-bees.

The first one offers a promise of loyalty to Jesus. Jesus offers the mysterious response about the Son of Man having nowhere to lay his head, suggesting that the road ahead was going to be tough for all who followed Jesus. The second disciple wanna-bee offers a plausible reason for the delay in responding to Jesus' call. He wants to wait until his father has died. And Jesus says, "Let the dead bury their own dead, but for you go and proclaim the Good News." The last one wants to follow Jesus but appeals to him to "let me first say farewell to those at my home." Jesus offers a foretaste of the gospel's absolute earnestness by saying, "No one who puts a hand to the plow and looks back is fit for the kingdom of God." Jesus is looking for followers who will commit to his urgent mission now, today. It's a matter for suitable, appropriate and capable disciples. It's not a matter of worthiness. It requires our complete focus and attention on the goal Jesus places before us. It requires a perfect effort on our part.

A perfect effort. I don't know about you, but I am far from perfect. Not even close. And unless I've missed my guess, you are far from perfect, too. How can we make our perfect effort for God?

The word perfect in this context is not about being faultless, flawless or impeccable. It's about being complete, being whole, well-rounded and entirely intact. So, it's really about making a complete effort for God and what God calls us to be in the world. It is not about living a perfect life but making an honest effort to grow and learn in the midst of adversity and challenge. In other words, to make a Perfect Effort is to give a complete effort in the midst of life's challenges and adversities to the Kingdom of God. Then and only then do we grow spiritually and grow in our faith.

God invites us to join in this endeavor and not to hesitate. Jesus gives us a glimpse into the gospel's absolute earnestness. This is the most important thing right now. It requires commitment, sacrifice and love for others. In fact, God's invitation to call us to God's ministry in Jesus Christ is so important that everything else pales in comparison. All is to be sacrificed for God kingdom. A perfect effort is required.

In our world we often look for shortcuts and bargains. We hedge our bets and play both ends against the middle. There was a time when your word was your bond. There was a time when you made a commitment and stuck with it. Today the world changes so much so fast it's hard to keep up with the changes. New mobile phones come out all the time. New studies come out regularly that too often contradict each other, leaving us wondering what to believe and follow.

We find this commitment to be too hard to maintain. We find it hard to keep our focus, to keep our eye on the prize, because such a commitment seems too radical, too far-fetched, too out-there. We prefer looking out for ourselves, our own interests, our own commitments.

The "perfect effort" vocabulary comes from a retired high school football coach named Bob Ladocaucer. He coached and taught at De La Salle High School in Concord, CA. Coach Lad holds the longest winning street all sports at every level: 151 games. Everyone on the outside who only saw the winning streak believed they were cheating to win. They thought he was cheating and breaking rules. But he wasn't. Coach Lad said the winning streak was never their goal. He focused on transforming boys into outstanding young men and good citizens using football as the vehicle to that end. It just so happened they won football games. Coach Lad stressed that love was like a glue that produced bonds of friendship and trust among the members of the team. The bonds that formed worked in these relationships building trust. Coach Lad's main goal was to raise up men who could be depended on.

The Good News is that Jesus the Christ commits himself fully and absolutely to you and me. God's love never ends; God's love for his creation is unwavering and never-ending. Our God is a God of relationship. And like any relationship, it's a two-way street; it takes two to tango, as my Dad used to say when I was growing up. God has made and continues to make a perfect effort in this relationship, whether we readily accept Jesus as Lord and Savior or not. The other half of the relationship is up to us. We must commit to making a perfect effort each and every day to be the disciples we are called to be.

God's love for us is unwavering. God reached out to each of us so that we made be in relationship with him.

As we follow Christ, we must make a perfect effort to be Christ's disciples; to totally commit all our time, talent and treasure to God.

A Baby Changes Everything
Isaiah 7:10-16

When a baby enters your life, everything changes. All bets are off. A new day has dawned. It all really starts before the baby enters the world. Before the birth of a baby, especially the first child, your calendar fills up quickly with regular doctor visits, setting up the child's room with the right furniture, colors and theme, the showering of gifts from loved ones and friends, and my personal favorite the childbirth preparation classes. We learned breathing and relaxation techniques, the stages of labor, and so much more. It was truly an experience.

A baby also changes how you travel. Can't just jump in the car and go anymore. You must place the baby in a 5-point harness car carrier or else you don't get to leave the hospital. The stereo system you love and enjoy gets moved and replaced by a pack-n-play. Your favorite chair is replaced by a mechanical swing. The crib, changing table, a dresser, child proofing everything, having storage for toys and books, and an eventual highchair in the kitchen: your home is transformed into a "baby cave"; your own Babies-R-Us store. I am amazed at how much additional gear is needed to travel with one little person.

There's the lack of regular, sound, deep sleep. There's the constant attention needed to attend to a baby's needs: changing diapers, getting them dressed, doing laundry, feeding the baby, getting the baby dressed again, getting yourself dressed again, doing more laundry. You get the idea.

And in the end, we do what we have to do when a baby enters our lives. Why? Because we love them more than we imagined we could love anyone. A baby is a sign of God's creative love and irresistible grace. A baby serves as a sign of God's love for the world and all creation and at the same time we, the parents, experience the love of God in a whole new way and our lives are changed forever. A baby is a sign of hope in a world of despair; a sign of peace in a world of violence; a sign of joy in a world of unhappiness; a sign of love in a world of hate.

We find ourselves this morning with King Ahaz in the middle of a foreign policy crisis, fearful of his two close neighbors to the north, Syria and Israel (vs. 4–6). The prophet has just warned King Ahaz that only faith will rescue the king from this apparent threat (vs. 7–9).

God invites King Ahaz, the king of Judah, to ask for a sign, but he refuses. God wanted him to ask for any kind of a sign because God wanted to prove to Ahaz that He would protect him from the kings of Syria and Ephraim. But Ahaz refused to ask for a sign because he really wanted to ask help from Assyria and continue practicing idolatry. The point of the sign is to underscore God's intention to do as he promised.

We're always looking for signs, but we don't always see them, or we refuse to see them. We look for them in the mall, when driving in unfamiliar neighborhoods, when looking for a bathroom in a restaurant or when checking into a hotel (where's the fitness room, the swimming pool, the business center?). We look for signs when deplaning and wandering through the airport terminal ("Where do I catch my connecting flight? Where's baggage claim? What carousel number?"), but in the hustle and bustle of a busy airport it's easy to miss a sign and go in the wrong direction. Or when hiking on a trail in the mountains, following the trail signs when you notice they are worn out, simply missing and difficult to discern. When life isn't going our way, we look for signs of improvement and growth from God. Noah looked for a sign and God gave him a rainbow in the sky. The Hebrews looked for signs and received manna from heaven in the morning, quails in their camps in the evening, and water from the rock. The shepherds living in the fields keeping watch over their flocks by night received a sign that in the city of David they would find a child wrapped in bands of cloth and lying in a manger who is the savior of the world.

The king's refusal is wrapped up in some form of personal piety. The clever but stubborn refusal of the king evokes from the prophet a hard, devastating oracle (vs. 13–17). The prophet Isaiah puts the royal Ahaz administration on notice. The prophet now refers to Yahweh as "my God." By implication, this odd pronoun suggests that Yahweh is no longer "your God." Yahweh has withdrawn from the dynasty. The dynasty wanted autonomy, and now it has it, for the Davidic house no longer is claimed by God. "Therefore" (v. 14), because of the king's resistance, the prophet announces a "sign", even though the king has not asked for one. The sign is that a young woman will have a child (v. 14). All the focus in the oracle is on the anticipated baby whose name is Immanuel, "God is with us" (v. 14). The birth and growth of the baby present a timeline to the nations: "Before the child knows how to refuse the evil and choose the good" is commonly calculated in terms of childhood development as two years. Before two years, the threat of Syria and Israel will dissolve (v. 16). That's the good news. The bad news is that with the disappearance of these small kings whom Ahaz so much fears, Yahweh will "bring on you" bad, bad days.

Is it any wonder that we should be looking for signs to guide us on our spiritual journey? That's the way we're wired. And especially at Advent!

What signs are you looking for? Is it a sign to confirm a sense of new calling in your life? Perhaps it's a sign that comes from a doctor visit or a trusted loved one saying it's time to change your unhealthy habits or you will die. Or is it simply a word of hope? A feeling of peace? An experience of joy? The power of love? A bright star shining in the east? The Christ child lying in an animal feeding trough?

The sign of the Christ child, the sign of Emmanuel, changes everything. Everything changes when "God is with us".

The power of the Immanuel sign calls us to live faithfully in God's promise to always be with us. The Emmanuel sign calls us to have the courage of faith to test that promise when we are challenged by the enemy.

The challenge of the Immanuel sign is stated by the prophet to King Ahaz in v. 9: "If you do not stand firm in faith, you shall not stand at all". Stand firm in your faith as we cry out to God, "O Come, O Come Emmanuel and ransom captive Israel, that mourns in lonely exile here, until the son of God appear…come and cheer our spirits by Thine advent here; disperse the gloomy clouds of night, and death's dark shadows put to flight…bind all peoples in one heart and mind; bid envy, strife and discord cease; fill the whole world with heaven's peace. Rejoice! Rejoice! Emmanuel, God is with us, shall come to thee."

Get ready! Everything changes when "God is with us"! Amen.

Outliers, Inc.

Malachi 3:1-4; Luke 3:1-6

Have you ever noticed that events in life, such as untimely deaths or political scandals, tend to come in threes? Michael Jackson's untimely death was followed by the death of Ed McMahon and Farrah Fawcett that same week. Buddy Holly, Ritchie Valens and the "Big Bopper" all died together in a plane crash in 1959. Jimmy Hendrix, Janice Joplin and Jim Morrison all died within weeks of each other in 1970. Former Governors Eliot Spitzer, Jim McGreevey and Mark Sanford all resigned their elected offices because extramarital affairs. Did you also know that in a group of 23 people, there is a 50 percent probability that two of them will share a birthday, not necessarily in the same year. The rule of 3 is a powerful one. In baseball, three strikes and you're out and three outs and the inning is over. How about this: we can go three minutes without breathing, three days without water, and three weeks without food. The Trinity comes in three: Father, Son and Holy Spirit. The genetic code, the code for life, is based on a trinity of nucleotides each specifying the nature of exactly one amino acid. Three is the magic number.

John's appearance on the scene a couple millennia ago followed a 400-year period often known as the "silent years," i.e., the period of time between the end of the Old Testament and the beginning of the New Testament. In that period of time, there'd been no major prophetic activity.

Suddenly, things get interesting! The rule of three comes into focus. First, "the word of God came to John son of Zechariah in the wilderness," so our text says. John bursts forth into the region around the Jordan River like he's swinging a baseball bat, looking for the fences: "... proclaiming a baptism of repentance for the forgiveness of sins," and his hearers quickly conclude that the time of prophetic silence is over. As another gospel writer tells it (John 1:19-23), once John makes clear that he is not himself the Messiah, the crowd immediately concludes that perhaps he is the return of Elijah or "the prophet" (a Moses-like figure, predicted to come; see Deuteronomy 18:15). But John accepts neither of those identities, describing himself only as "the voice of one crying out in the wilderness," a quote from Isaiah. But no matter how John describes himself, the people hear him as a prophetic voice from God. Jesus later calls John a prophet, too (Matthew 11:9).

Then comes along another prophet! First comes John, and then comes Jesus himself. Jesus appears on the scene, more than a prophet, to be sure, but the crowds recognized the prophetic in him as well (see Matthew 21:11). Jesus even called himself a prophet on one occasion (Luke 4:24).

And then, not too much later, along comes Paul! Nobody seems to have called him a prophet per se, but the Lord described Paul's work to Ananias in prophet-like terms, calling him "an instrument whom I have chosen to bring my name before Gentiles and kings and before the people of Israel" (Acts 9:15).

So what's going on here? No prophets of great stature for 400 years, and suddenly there are three!? Those three, to use a term from statistics, were outliers, which refers to something (or someone) situated away from the main group. That is, John, Jesus and Paul were prophets in a way quite different from others who also bore that title during the same time period.

Why is this important?

Because ... of the message these outliers brought to the world. There's a divine agenda behind what happens in the world. John's main call was for a baptism of repentance for the forgiveness of sins; the ritual of cleansing, signifying a return to God with the expectation of forgiveness. In other words, what makes this so important is that the first thing people needed to do was to align themselves with God's plan by repenting and receiving forgiveness for their sins.

Malcolm Gladwell, a former business and science reporter for The Washington Post, addressed this Prophet Clustering or Genius Clustering in his best-selling book Outliers. His research suggests that high IQ itself is overrated and that many people are smart enough to succeed when they have cultural advantages and given the right opportunities -- meaning that they are in the right place at the right time as certain historical developments are occurring. Gladwell says it this way: "The people who stand before kings may look like they did it all by themselves. But in fact they are invariably the beneficiaries of hidden advantages and extraordinary opportunities and cultural legacies that allow them to learn and work hard and make sense of the world in ways others cannot. It makes a difference where and when we grew up".

As an example, in his book Gladwell points out that Bill Joy, Bill Gates, Steve Jobs, Paul Allen, Steve Ballmer, Scott McNealy and Eric Schmidt, all power-players in the U.S. computer industry, were all born between 1953 and 1956. Gladwell explains this by noting that Silicon Valley veterans agree that the most important date in the history of the personal computer revolution was January 1975, the month when the magazine Popular Mechanics ran a cover story about the Altair 8800, a desktop computer you could build from a kit at home. This was a significant departure from the huge mainframes that were up to that point the only computers available and were so expensive that only corporations, government agencies and universities could afford them. But now, here was a $397 computer kit you could assemble in your garage.

Gladwell argues that those in the best position to take advantage of this breakthrough were people born between 1953 and 1956. Those in Silicon Valley interested in computers but born before those dates had jobs at IBM, which made mainframes. Once you were part of the mainframe industry, you saw little value in pathetic desktop machines. You belonged to a different paradigm. Likewise, those born after those dates were simply too young to get in on the ground level of the personal-computing revolution.

In other words, it isn't that there aren't people just as smart as Bill Gates, Steve Jobs and Bill Joy born in the several years before and after them, it is that the same opportunity wasn't available to them.

Now apply all of this to the Jewish population of the first-century Roman Empire. Obviously Jesus, as the Son of God, is a special case, and I am not suggesting that given the right timing of birth and the right placement geographically, any smart Jewish child could have become the Messiah. But we can take this business of opportunity and cultural legacy to mean that many born in the years before or after Jesus and John (and perhaps Paul -- we don't know when he was born) had the potential to become great prophets, too, had the timing been right.

When John first preached in the region around the Jordan, his primary concern was not with everybody treating one another nicely or following the Ten Commandments or fighting for justice for all. John's main calling was for a baptism of repentance for the forgiveness of sins; to align themselves with God's plan by repenting and receiving forgiveness for their sins.

Author C.S. Lewis describes the unrepentant condition as being in a "hole" where we need the help of a friend (i.e., a savior) to get us out. And what sort of hole is it we've gotten ourselves into? For one thing, it's behaving as if we belonged to ourselves. We are not simply imperfect creatures who need improvement; we are rebels who must lay down our arms. "Laying down your arms, surrendering, saying you are sorry, realizing that you have been on the wrong track and getting ready to start life over again from the ground floor -- that is the only way out of a 'hole,'" says Lewis. And this process of surrender is what we call repentance (the Greek "changing the mind" or "turning around"), and it's what John was calling for in his prophetic preaching.

Lewis adds this important note: "... this repentance ... is not something God demands of you before he will take you back and which he could let you off if he chose: it is simply a description of what going back to him is like." We cannot be right with God without repentance; it's like asking God to take us back without actually going back.

In October 1989, the city of San Francisco was struck by a powerful earthquake. Huge cracks appeared in the walls of Candlestick Park, where thousands of fans were waiting to watch the third game of the World Series. Sections of freeway twisted and buckled; some collapsed. At least twenty-seven fires broke out across the city; the largest, in the Marina District, consumed dozens of buildings.

At the edge of the Marina District, a crowd of curiosity-seekers gathered, watching the firefighters as they battled the flames. After a few minutes of this, a police officer came up to the crowd and began shouting at them. "What have you come to look at?" he said to them. "This is no time to be standing around. There's been an earthquake. You all have work to do! Go home. Fill your bathtubs with water (if you still have water). Prepare yourselves to live for the next several days without electricity. The sun's going to set in another hour; your time is running out. The firefighters will do their job here: Now you go home and do yours!"

That police officer spoke truth, as John the Baptist spoke truth. He spoke with urgency, as John the Baptist spoke with urgency. His message, like John's, was what the people truly needed to hear.

What's the message we most need to hear, in these ever-shortening days of Advent? Is it a message of spending and partying and conspicuous consumption? Or is it a message of repentance and forgiveness and faithfulness?

During this Advent season, in what wilderness should our voice be crying out? Where are we needed to proclaim a baptism of repentance? It's where we play, where we work; it's in our schools, in our homes, downtown, out in the country, on the highways and the by-ways. We must proclaim this before the seats of power and influence at the courthouse and the statehouse; the White House and the Congressional house. We must proclaim that all people, no matter their race, gender, ethnicity or creed, must repent of our sinful nature and get right with God. In the words of John Donne, "No man is an island...we are all part of the main...". We are all in this together.

Malcolm Gladwell also writes, "It's impossible for ... any ... outlier ... to look down from their lofty perch and say with truthfulness, 'I did this all by myself.' Superstar lawyers and math whizzes and software entrepreneurs appear at first blush to lie outside ordinary experience. But they don't. They are products of history and community, of opportunity and legacy. Their success is not exceptional or mysterious. It is grounded in a web of advantages and inheritance, some deserved, some not, some earned, some just plain lucky

--- but all critical to making them who they are. The outlier, in the end, is not an outlier at all."

John, Jesus and Paul indeed were a genius cluster. Jesus, of course, is unique because of his divine identity, but, if the outlier research is correct, given the right timing of birth and upbringing in a culture steeped in the Old Testament, many of us might have been able to fulfill the roles John and Paul did in the introduction of Christ to the world. That time has passed, of course, but there is still the opportunity to introduce Christ to new generations, and to tell them of repentance, the path to getting right with God. We can be a John or Paul to those who haven't yet understood that.

In addition to the scriptural references, these sources were frequently used in the development of this book:

· "1001 Quotes, Illustrations & Humorous Stories for Preachers, Teachers & Writers" from Edward K. Rowell & Leadership Journal (Grand Rapids: Baker Books, 1996-1997). Permission to copy. · Kaylor, Bob and Merrill, Timothy www.homileticsonline.com. n.d. subscriber since 2011.

· Interpretation: A Bible Commentary for Teaching and Preaching, Ed. by James L. Mays, Patrick D. Miller, and Paul J. Achtemeier (Louisville: John Knox Press, 1990).

· The Daily Study Bible Series, Revised Edition, Trans. and Ed. by William Barclay (Philadelphia: The Westminster Press, 1975).

CPSIA information can be obtained
at www.ICGtesting.com
Printed in the USA
BVHW041144081019
560527BV00012B/82/P